THE PMP Project Management Professional Certification Exams

By

Ace5

This book is published by BC Seminary Publishers.

Kindle Edition

FIRST EDITION: 2023

ISBN: 978-1-961902-23-7

Contents

Introduction

Navigating the complex landscape of project management can often feel like deciphering a foreign script. Technical jargons, intricate methodologies, and layers of processes — it's a maze that many have lost themselves in. This is especially true when preparing for the PMP Project Management Professional Certification Exam. There's no shortage of guides and manuals out there, each more complex and denser than the last. Yet, every aspiring professional yearns for that one resource that can make sense of it all, without overwhelming them.

Enter this book.

Our aim has never been to add to the pile of perplexing literature that seems to be growing exponentially. Instead, we've chosen a different path: to simplify. In these pages, you won't be bombarded with technical overload or superfluous details. This book is designed to be your compass, pointing you in the right direction and providing you with just the right amount of information — neither too little nor too much.

Think of this guide as the 'Goldilocks' of PMP preparation: it's just right.

We've distilled decades of project management wisdom, experiences from countless professionals, and feedback from students into a guide that is accessible, practical, and above all, simple. Our aim is to take you from curious novice to confident professional, ready to tackle the PMP exam and emerge victorious.

In a world where complexity is often mistaken for depth, this book stands apart. Welcome to a simpler, more effective way to prepare for the PMP Certification Exam. Welcome to clarity amidst chaos.

Chapter 1: The PMP Certification Basics

The Project Management Professional (PMP) certification is a globally recognized credential offered by the Project Management Institute (PMI). Earning the PMP certification signifies a commitment to project management excellence. This designation is highly sought after by employers and individuals alike, as it can lead to increased earning potential, career advancement, and recognition within the industry.

Why PMP?

1. **Global Recognition:** The PMP is acknowledged worldwide. This certification opens doors to global job opportunities in project management.
2. **Higher Earnings:** Multiple surveys have shown that PMP-certified professionals often earn more than their non-certified counterparts.
3. **Skill Enhancement:** Preparing for the PMP exam itself hones your project management skills. It covers a comprehensive curriculum that equips you for real-world challenges.
4. **Employer Preference:** Many organizations now make the PMP certification a prerequisite for project management roles.

Eligibility Criteria: Before embarking on the PMP journey, it's important to know if you're eligible.

1. **Education:** At a minimum, you should have a secondary degree (high school diploma or the global equivalent).
2. **Professional Experience:** With a secondary degree, you need at least five years of project management experience with 7,500 hours leading projects. If you have a four-year degree (bachelor's degree or global equivalent), you only need three years of project management experience with 4,500 hours leading projects.
3. **Training:** Irrespective of your academic qualifications, 35 contact hours of formal project management education is a must.

Exam Structure: The PMP exam is rigorous, covering various aspects of project management spread across different process groups and knowledge areas. Here's a basic structure:

1. **Number of Questions:** 180 questions (of which about

175 are scored, and 5 are pre-test unscored).

2. **Duration:** 230 minutes.
3. **Format:** Multiple Choice, Multiple Responses, Matching, Hotspot, and Limited Fill-in-the-Blank.

The questions are based on the PMI's "A Guide to the Project Management Body of Knowledge (PMBOK® Guide)". This guide is a comprehensive book that covers the core principles of project management.

Preparation Tips:

1. **Understand the PMBOK Guide:** This is your bible for the exam. Make sure to read and understand the processes, knowledge areas, and the intricate network of process inputs, tools, techniques, and outputs.
2. **Practice with Mock Exams:** Simulated exams give you a feel of the real thing. Time yourself and get accustomed to the exam pattern.
3. **Join a Study Group:** Sharing knowledge and discussing challenging topics with peers can be invaluable.
4. **Stay Updated:** PMI frequently updates the exam based on the changes in the industry. Ensure you're studying the latest version of the PMBOK Guide and that your training materials are up to date.

The PMP certification is a significant achievement and a testament to one's dedication and expertise in the project management field. While the journey to earning the certification may be demanding, the rewards in terms of career growth, earning potential, and professional recognition make it well worth the effort. As with any challenging endeavor, thorough preparation is the key. Equip yourself with the right resources, strategies, and mindset to ace the exam and elevate your project management career.

Remember, while the PMP certification is a stepping stone, the real-world experience, continuous learning, and adaptability will define your success in the ever-evolving world of project management. Good luck to all the aspiring candidates!

PMP fundamentals

Although there are certain abilities that every successful project manager must have, many companies just promote their technical specialists to management positions. It is assumed incorrectly that their level of experience in their technical domains translates to project management. The opposite is also possible. Managers of projects are multi-talented generalists. They may wear many hats and are creative problem solvers.

While technical expertise is a useful asset, it is not necessary for successful project management. There should be a few technical specialists on your project team; the manager may then consult with them about the finer technical points. Aspiring project managers may advance their careers by learning and adopting sound project management practices, as well as by developing their knowledge of strategic and business management and their interpersonal abilities.

Some have compared project managers to entrepreneurs. They need to have a basic understanding of all facets of management. General management encompasses all facets of management, including but not limited to accounting, strategic planning, supervision, and human resource management. Communication, leadership, and the ability to make sound decisions are just a few examples of the "soft skills" that go under the umbrella term of "interpersonal abilities."

Every undertaking requires the use of general management and people abilities. However, expertise in a particular field of application may be necessary for certain projects. The term "application areas" refers to groups of related initiatives. These components, or domains of use, may be classified in a number of ways, including by kind of business (automotive, pharmaceutical), by function (accounting, marketing), and by area of expertise (software engineering, electrical engineering, procurement, R&D).

Disciplines, laws, and the unique requirements of the project, the client, or the industry are typical topics of interest in these sorts of applications. For instance, the construction sector is not subject to the same procurement regulations that apply to government projects. Regulations established by the Food and Drug Administration are of utmost importance to the pharmaceutical business. The auto industry could care less about these two sorts of rules. Project management skills will benefit greatly from prior expertise in the field of application in which you are working.

Even if you plan to bring in specialists in the relevant fields, it is still helpful to have a basic understanding of those fields. Project managers are not required to know everything or execute every job on a project. However, they should have the necessary technical knowledge and expertise to handle the scope, difficulty, and danger of the project.

In addition to their other duties, they promote the PMO's success and benefits and act as advocates for the importance of project management. The PMBOK ® Guide specifies the PMI® Talent TriangleTM, which includes technical project management abilities, leadership skills, and strategic and business management skills, as necessary for every project manager. Next, I'll go through each of them individually, along with several additional abilities that I think form the backbone of effective project management. The success (or failure) of the project may depend on how well you handle them. We'll take a high-level look at these abilities now;

Skills in Project Management Technology

When discussing project management, the term "technical skills" refers to the specific abilities required to carry out the job. The ability to define the project's important success criteria, create a workable project timeline, recognize when you don't know something and seek advice, and know when to ask for assistance are all part of this category of abilities.

As I said before, the project manager is not expected to be the technical expert (with respect to the project's end result), and there should be enough subject matter experts on the team to deal with technical issues. The project manager's main concerns include the project's timeline, budget, resources, and hazards, as well as the proper use of relevant tools and procedures. The PMI ® Talent TriangleTM includes technical competencies in project management.

Strategic thinking and business management

Managers of projects should be able to explain how the project's requirements relate to the organization's overall objectives in terms of things like operations, market circumstances, competition, and strategy. This also implies that the project manager should have a fundamental familiarity with the interconnections between the project's objectives and the company's financial, marketing, customer service, and production processes.

Knowing the organization's business goals and its long-term vision will help you choose which project components are most important to keep an eye on and which deliveries can wait. Knowing how to manage the project's scope and timeline, as well as the risks and challenges involved in bringing about the project's outcomes, is an essential part of every businessperson's toolkit.

You should also be familiar with the ins and outs of the organization's politics and, most crucially, with the people who hold the reins when it comes to getting things done for your project. The PMI ® Talent TriangleTM encompasses abilities in business management and strategy. Excellent communication skills are one of the most essential qualities of a successful project manager. Successful initiatives always have strong written and spoken communications. Throughout the course of your project, a wide variety of channels of contact will be available.

It is your responsibility as the project's primary communicator (project documentation, meeting updates, status reports, etc.) to ensure that all information conveyed is thorough, accurate, and easy to follow. Once the knowledge has been disseminated, it is up to the recipients to ensure its comprehension.

Capacity for Planning and Organization

A project manager's ability to organize and plan is strongly tied to, and maybe even more vital than, their ability to communicate effectively. There are several approaches to organization. As a project manager, you'll need to keep track of and quickly retrieve a wide variety of documents, including those pertaining to project specifications, internal memoranda, status reports, employee files, vendor quotations, and contracts. Depending on the nature of the project, you may also need to manage and plan media-release schedules, have regular meetings, and assemble appropriate teams. Organizational competence is intrinsically linked to proficiency in time management.

Without knowing how you're spending your time, it's tough to keep things in order. If you've never gone to a class like this before, I highly suggest it. They provide useful advice on how to organize your day, deal with distractions, and prioritize tasks. Throughout this book, I talk a lot about planning. Nothing about managing a project can be done without first engaging in some kind of planning. Skills in organizing are useless without the companion skill of planning.

If you have both of these and can communicate well, you will go far in the area of project management. A Capable Handle On Conflict Give me a project, and I'll show you the conflicts. Problems are inevitable in every undertaking, as they are in other aspects of life. That's supposed to be what makes people strong, right? In any case, I stray from my point.

Managing conflicts is all about finding solutions. There are two sides to every problem. Identifying the root of the issue is the first step in finding a solution. When trying to define an issue, it's easy to become stuck explaining the symptoms rather than the underlying cause. To keep from doing so, you should inquire as to whether the issue is coming from inside or outside. Have we run across a technical snag? Is there tension amongst those working on this project? Has a supervisory role been established? What are the probable results or effects? Asking inquiries like these will lead you to the root of the issue. After you have identified the issue, you will need to select a few choices. It will take some time to investigate the root of the issue and determine the best course of action.

The project manager will next analyze the results and decide on the best course of action. It's not only the choice itself that matters, but the timing of it. Making a smart choice but putting it into action too late might lead to regret. Ability to negotiate and persuade others is essential for successful issue resolution. Every day, in some way, we all use our negotiating talents. I get asked, "Honey, what do you want for dinner?" every single night. Then the bargaining starts, and you have to decide between fried chicken and swordfish. Negotiation, in its most basic sense, is working with other people to reach a compromise. Almost every aspect of a project requires negotiation, including but not limited to its scope, budget, contracts, resource allocations, and more. This might happen many times during the project and may entail individual or group negotiations.

If the other person really wants fried chicken, you may influence them to have swordfish instead. The capacity to get things done through influencing other people counts, too. To effectively exert influence, you must be familiar with the official and informal organizational structures of all the groups working on the project. Politics and power are instruments for getting what you want out of others. Power is the power to coerce others into doing actions they otherwise would not take. It's the power to persuade others and alter the way things are going.

Politics is the art of inspiring factions with divergent goals to work together ingeniously despite the presence of conflict and anarchy. These abilities will be put to use in every facet of managing projects. Get some early practice in, since you'll definitely be using these abilities in your future endeavor.

Ability to Lead

Managers and leaders are two different roles. Leaders inspire and motivate their followers by sharing their vision, building agreement on strategic objectives, and establishing the path forward.

They help lead the group to success by pointing them in the right direction. Managers care mostly about the end product and about completing the task in accordance with the specifications. Project managers need to demonstrate the traits of both leaders and managers at certain points during the project. It takes a highly tuned and vital skill to know when to go from leadership to management and back again. The talent of leadership is a part of the Talent TriangleTM.

Competence in Inspiring Others and Building Teams

Managers of large projects will need to excel in inspiring and building cohesive teams. Teams often consist of employees from various departments. The project manager may need to facilitate certain team-building activities, depending on whether or not the individuals have previously collaborated. The project manager is responsible for establishing the group's culture and guiding its members through the team building process to achieve peak performance. The project manager also plays a crucial role in keeping the team motivated throughout the duration of the project, which is particularly critical for lengthy projects or those that encounter many challenges.

An important nuance of the team-building function is that project managers are often tasked with inspiring team members who are not directly under their supervision. This situation has its own unique problems. If you want to assist, you may ask the functional manager to be included in the performance assessments of the people on your project team. Make sure you have a voice in this by use the bargaining and persuasion techniques I mentioned.

A Project Manager's Duties

The success of a project depends on the efforts of the project manager. Projects boost the company's worth since they provide tangible results. The worth of a business is the sum amount of its assets, both material and intangible.

The project manager's knowledge of the company's strategic strategy is essential for aligning the portfolio's projects with the company's long-term goals. All the knowledge from before must be used here. You've been exposed to some of the tools you'll need, so you can tackle your next project with confidence. These abilities include communication, problem-solving, leadership, and negotiation.

Knowing How Organizations Are Set Up

Organizations that carry out projects are as diverse as the projects themselves. Each company has its own unique culture, set of communication norms, and working methods that all play a role in how projects are carried out and whether or not they are successful. Since every company's culture is different, a wide variety of management styles may be found within them.

According to the PMBOK® Guide, the following are some of the factors that assist shape an organization's structure:

- Consistency with overall business goals
- Abilities, Proficiencies, and Competencies
- Path to escalation
- Hierarchical structure
- Degrees of duty and accountability
- Capacity for change
- Efficiency and effectiveness in operation
- Cost
- Places
- Transmissions

Organizational structures might be basic, multi-departmental, functional, project-oriented, matrix, virtual, hybrid, or PMO, as described in the Project Management Body of Knowledge (PMBOK® Guide). Learning the ins and outs of the company you work for may help you do your job more effectively.

Risky initiatives are more likely to be undertaken by companies with aggressive cultures that are content to be at the forefront of their respective industry. Managers of such projects should expect a warm reaction if they are prepared to provide novel ideas and initiatives that have never been tried before. Contrarily, hazardous ventures are unlikely to be undertaken by organizations with risk-averse cultures that want to follow the industry leader. Risk-taking, aggressive project managers are unlikely to be well-received in such an environment. How much power upper management is ready to give project managers might be an indicator of the sort of company you work for.

The organizational structure and the project manager's contacts with different levels of management indicate the scope of the manager's authority. A project manager, for instance, has very little sway in a purely functional company. Project manager is only one possible job title; they may also be known as a project leader, project coordinator, or project expeditor. And a project manager's degree of authority is often lower when working with managers at the operations level as opposed to those at the middle or strategic levels.

Requirements for the PMP

The Project Management Professional (PMP) certification, offered by the Project Management Institute (PMI), is one of the most esteemed credentials in the project management field. Earning this certification signifies a deep understanding of project management principles and practices. But before diving into the examination process, it's essential to understand the prerequisites needed to qualify.

1. Educational Background
Your education plays a role in determining the amount of professional experience you'll need:

- **Secondary Degree (High school diploma, associate's degree, or equivalent):** If you fall into this category, you'll need more hands-on project management experience to qualify for the exam.
- **Four-Year Degree (Bachelor's degree or equivalent):** With a bachelor's degree or higher, the required project management experience is reduced.

2. Project Management Experience

The core requirement for the PMP is hands-on experience leading and directing projects:

- **Secondary Degree Holders:** You need to have accumulated 7,500 hours of leading and directing projects.
- **Four-Year Degree Holders:** You need to have accrued 4,500 hours of leading and directing projects.

This experience should be spread across the five project management processes: initiating, planning, executing, monitoring & controlling, and closing. It's crucial to maintain detailed records of your project management experience as PMI might ask you to provide this evidence if your application is audited.

3. Project Management Education
Regardless of your formal education or job experience, you also need 35 contact hours of project management education. These hours can come from PMI-authorized training providers, PMI chapters, employer-sponsored programs, or even university/college academic programs. Online courses, workshops, and training sessions count as long as they're related to project management and you can provide evidence of completion.

4. Application Process

Once you've met the above requirements:

- **Complete the Online Application:** PMI's online certification system guides you through the process. Be accurate and thorough when detailing your project management experience.
- **Pass an Audit (if selected):** A percentage of applications are randomly selected for audit. If chosen, you'll need to provide evidence of your claimed education and experience.

5. Examination

The PMP exam itself tests your competency in project management. It consists of 200 multiple-choice questions, and candidates have 4 hours to complete it. It covers the domains of project management, from initiation to closing, and requires a deep understanding of both the theoretical and practical aspects.

6. Maintaining Your PMP Certification

Once you've earned the PMP credential, your journey doesn't end there. To retain your certification, you need to stay updated and involved in the project management community.

- **Earn 60 PDUs (Professional Development Units) every three years:** PDUs are hours spent on professional development and learning activities related to project management. There are various ways to earn PDUs, such as attending PMI seminars, webinars, or other educational sessions; participating in professional research; or even teaching others about project management. The idea is to ensure PMPs stay current and evolve with the ever-changing landscape of project management.

7. Examination Content and Focus Areas

Understanding the exam's structure is vital. The PMP exam tests on several domains:

- **Initiating (13%):** This encompasses the processes performed to define a new project or a new phase of an existing project.
- **Planning (24%):** This domain focuses on establishing the total scope of the effort, defining and refining the objectives, and developing the course of action required to achieve those objectives.
- **Executing (31%):** It covers the processes performed to complete the work defined in the project management

plan and to satisfy the project specifications.

- **Monitoring and Controlling (25%)**: Here, the emphasis is on tracking, reviewing, and regulating the progress and performance of the project, ensuring that you keep the project on track and manage any changes that might occur.
- **Closing (7%)**: This pertains to the processes performed to finalize all activities and formally close the project.

Each domain has its set of tasks, knowledge, and skills that will be tested.

8. **Preparation Techniques**

To excel in the PMP exam:

- **Comprehensive Study Plan:** Start by creating a structured plan outlining your study routine. Stick to it, making adjustments as needed.
- **Mock Exams:** Regularly take full-length practice tests to familiarize yourself with the exam format and assess your readiness.
- **Study Groups:** Collaborating with peers can offer different perspectives and shared resources, enhancing your understanding.
- **Engage with the PMI community:** Attending PMI chapter meetings,

workshops, or seminars can expose you to valuable insights from seasoned PMPs.

9. **Resources**

While PMI's **PMBOK (Project Management Body of Knowledge)** Guide is a foundational resource, consider complementing it with other PMP exam prep books and tools, which offer diverse strategies, practice questions, and insights.

The overview provided encompasses the key requirements and considerations for the PMP certification. However, the world of project management is vast, and the PMP exam is comprehensive. Here are a few more critical points and tips that prospective candidates might find beneficial:

10. **Understand the PMBOK Guide's Framework**

The **PMBOK Guide** introduces you to the standardized processes, best practices, terminologies, and guidelines of project management. It's important to:

- Familiarize yourself with the **10 Knowledge Areas**: These are the core disciplines of project management, from Project Integration Management to Project Stakeholder Management.
- Understand the **49 Processes** spread across these knowledge areas and the five Process Groups

(Initiating, Planning, Executing, Monitoring & Controlling, Closing).

- Dive deep into the **Inputs, Tools & Techniques, and Outputs (ITTOs)** for each process.

11. Continuous Learning

Stay updated with PMI's official publications, blogs, and forums. Engage with online communities like **ProjectManagement.com**, which is affiliated with PMI and offers webinars, articles, and discussions that can earn you PDUs.

12. Physical and Mental Preparedness

As you approach the exam:

- **Rest Well**: Ensure you get a good night's sleep before the exam.
- **Stay Calm**: Use relaxation techniques to manage anxiety.
- **Time Management**: During the exam, watch the clock. While you need to ensure you attempt every question, spending too much time on any single one can be detrimental.
- **Read Every Question Thoroughly**: Sometimes, the difference between the correct and incorrect answer can hinge on a single word or phrase.

13. Post-Certification

Once you're PMP certified, flaunt it! Add it to your resume, LinkedIn profile, and business cards. The PMP designation can open doors to new job opportunities, higher earning potential, and professional respect.

While the details provided are extensive, it's essential to recognize that each candidate's journey to PMP certification is unique. Tailor your preparation to your learning style, experience, and the resources available to you. The journey is demanding but deeply rewarding for those passionate about project management

The Professional Certification

Professional certifications, such as the Project Management Professional (PMP), are more than mere titles or credentials. They embody a blend of expertise, dedication, and distinction in a specialized field. As we delve deeper into the essence of 'The Professional Certification', let's use the PMP as our guiding star.

At its core, a professional certification is a validation from a recognized body that an individual has showcased an exemplary standard of expertise and aptitude in a particular domain. It differs from academic degrees, focusing more on specific, actionable skills than broad foundational theory.

The Essence of a Professional Certification

In the intricate tapestry of professional growth and career development, professional certifications emerge as distinct, shimmering threads. They are more than just markers on a resume; they are symbolic representations of an individual's commitment, expertise, and readiness for specific challenges in their chosen domain.

1. A Testament to Mastery:

Professional certifications validate an individual's competence in a specific area. By achieving this certification, one has not only acquired the necessary knowledge but has demonstrated, under rigorous evaluation, an ability to apply it effectively. It's a testimony to their dedication to mastering the intricate nuances of their profession.

2. Bridging Theory and Practice:

While traditional academic pathways provide foundational knowledge, professional certifications focus on the applied aspect of this knowledge. They emphasize real-world scenarios, problem-solving, and the practical application of theoretical constructs, ensuring a candidate is job-ready and equipped to handle industry-specific challenges.

3. A Continuous Learning Journey:

Earning a certification isn't the end; it's a significant milestone in a continuous journey of learning. Many professional certifications require periodic renewals, which necessitates ongoing education. This dynamic ensures professionals stay updated with the ever-evolving trends, tools, and best practices in their industry.

4. Global Recognition and Standardization:

In a globalized world, professional certifications often serve as universal markers of expertise. They transcend regional boundaries and offer a standardized benchmark, ensuring that a certified professional in one part of the world meets the same rigorous standards as another in a different region.

5. Enhanced Career Prospects:

In competitive job markets, certifications act as differentiators. They not only increase one's eligibility for diverse roles but also potentially elevate earning potentials. Recruiters and employers view certifications as evidence of a candidate's commitment to their profession and their readiness to take on challenging roles.

6. Fostering Professional Communities:

Certifications often come with membership to professional bodies or associations. Such affiliations provide networking opportunities, access to industry events, and a platform to share knowledge, fostering a sense of community and collaboration among like-minded professionals.

7. Personal Growth and Confidence:

Beyond the professional realm, the journey towards achieving a certification fosters personal growth. The rigorous preparation instills discipline, perseverance, and resilience. Successfully earning the certification boosts self-confidence, reinforcing the belief in one's capabilities.

The essence of a professional certification lies in its holistic value – to the individual, the industry, and the broader professional community. It's more than just an accolade; it's a reflection of an individual's passion for excellence, their drive to continuously evolve, and their commitment to their profession. As the professional landscape continues to shift and evolve, these certifications will remain steadfast beacons, guiding individuals towards avenues of growth, recognition, and success.

The Multifaceted Rewards of Certification

Professional certifications, especially those as rigorous and globally recognized as the PMP, yield benefits that extend far beyond a mere qualification on a resume. These rewards, intertwined and multifaceted, span across personal, professional, and industry-wide spectrums.

1. Personal Empowerment and Growth:

- **Intellectual Enrichment:** Aspiring towards certifications often requires deep dives into specific subject matters, broadening horizons and adding layers to an individual's intellectual foundation.

- **Confidence Boost:** Successfully navigating the rigors of certification programs bestows a sense of achievement. This boosts self-confidence, paving the way for greater professional risks and initiatives.
- **Lifelong Learning:** The journey to certification fosters a culture of continual learning, emphasizing the importance of staying updated and relevant in one's field.

2. **Professional Trajectory and Advancement:**

- **Competitive Advantage:** In a saturated job market, a recognized certification like the PMP offers differentiation. It's a signal to potential employers of both the candidate's commitment to the field and their mastery over it.
- **Career Mobility:** Certifications can be a catalyst for career growth, unlocking doors to leadership roles, international assignments, and high-profile projects.
- **Salary Enhancements:** Multiple surveys and studies have consistently shown that certified professionals, especially PMP holders, tend to command higher salaries compared to their non-certified counterparts.

3. **Enhanced Professional Credibility:**

- **Validation of Expertise:** Certifications are, in essence, validations from reputable organizations attesting to an individual's expertise and skills. They assure stakeholders, clients, and employers of the holder's capabilities.
- **Ethical Standing:** Many certifications, including the PMP, require adherents to follow a code of ethics. This not only enhances the credibility of the holder but also provides a moral framework for professional conduct.

4. **Networking and Community Integration:**

- **Being Part of a Global Community:** Acquiring a certification like the PMP ushers individuals into a global community of like-minded professionals. This network can be invaluable for knowledge sharing, collaboration, and even job opportunities.
- **Access to Resources:** Membership in professional bodies, often a boon

accompanying certifications, provides access to a trove of resources—journals, webinars, workshops, and exclusive events tailored for continuous professional development.

5. Industry and Organizational Impact:

- **Driving Best Practices:** Certified professionals, equipped with the latest knowledge and trends, often act as change agents in organizations, driving best practices and optimizing processes.
- **Influencing Organizational Credibility:** Organizations boasting a significant number of certified professionals, especially in project management, are often perceived as more reliable and competent by clients and stakeholders.

In the world of project management, and indeed in many professional spheres, the rewards of certifications are manifold. They're not just personal accolades but symbols of dedication, competence, and a commitment to excellence. The ripple effects of such qualifications can be felt at individual, organizational, and industry levels, substantiating their

unparalleled significance in today's professional landscape

The Comprehensive Journey of Certification

In the realm of professional development, obtaining a certification, particularly one as coveted as the PMP, is not a mere destination but a profound journey. This expedition through knowledge landscapes, practical terrains, and self-discovery corridors is transformative and enlightening. Let's examine this journey more closely.

1. Foundational Learning and Knowledge Building:

Before embarking on any professional certification, it's essential to establish a robust foundation. This involves:

- **Structured Learning:** Availing formal training, courses, or workshops ensures one receives comprehensive and standardized knowledge on the subject.
- **Self-study:** The role of textbooks, academic journals, and case studies cannot be underestimated. For PMP, the PMBOK (Project Management Body of Knowledge) is an invaluable resource.

2. Experiential Learning and Practical Application:

Theory without practice is like a ship without a rudder. In project management:

- **Hands-on Experience:** It's essential to participate actively in real-world projects, understanding the nuances of team dynamics, stakeholder management, risk assessment, and other tangible aspects of project delivery.
- **Mentorship:** Engaging with seasoned professionals or mentors helps in gaining insights from their experiences, avoiding common pitfalls, and strategizing one's approach.

3. Networking and Community Engagement:

Being part of a professional community offers myriad benefits:

- **Knowledge Exchange:** Networking events, seminars, and conferences allow aspirants to exchange ideas, get answers to pressing questions, and explore different methodologies and practices.
- **Staying Updated:** The field of project management is ever-evolving. Being plugged into a network ensures one stays abreast of the latest trends, tools, and methodologies.

4. Evaluation and Self-assessment:

Understanding one's strengths and areas of improvement is pivotal:

- **Mock Tests:** Regularly taking simulated exams helps gauge one's preparation level and fine-tune study strategies.
- **Feedback:** Seeking feedback from peers or mentors on one's project management approach, or even on mock test performances, can provide valuable insights.

5. Continual Growth and Adaptation:

The journey doesn't end with obtaining the certification:

- **Professional Development Units (PDUs):** For PMP holders, PMI requires ongoing learning through PDUs, ensuring that certified professionals are always engaged in refining their skills.
- **Lifelong Learning:** The spirit of inquiry and the desire to keep learning is essential. Exploring advanced courses, participating in webinars, or even attending workshops becomes part of the continual growth narrative.

The journey towards a professional certification, especially in the dynamic world of project management, is both rigorous and rewarding. It's a holistic blend of structured learning, hands-on experience, community engagement, self-assessment, and perpetual growth. This odyssey not only equips aspirants with the skills and knowledge to excel in their field but also molds them into lifelong learners, ready to adapt and lead in an ever-changing professional landscape.

PMP: A Deep Dive into Excellence

The Project Management Professional (PMP) certification, administered by the Project Management Institute (PMI), is more than just a certification; it's an affirmation of one's mastery in the vast and nuanced domain of project management. Let's break down its elements and understand why it's often referred to as the "gold standard" in project management.

1. Historical Context and Global Recognition:

Established in the early 1980s by the PMI, the PMP has grown in stature and importance. Today, it's globally recognized, transcending industries, cultures, and geographies. This global recognition ensures that a PMP-certified professional can effectively work on projects anywhere in the world, speaking a universally understood language of project management.

2. A Comprehensive Curriculum:

The PMP certification isn't narrowly focused. It covers the entire gamut of project management:

- **Project Integration Management:** Ensuring various components of the projects work in harmony.
- **Scope Management:** Defining and managing what is and isn't included in the project.
- **Schedule, Cost, and Quality Management:** Planning timelines, budgets, and ensuring the deliverables meet set standards.
- **Resource and Communications Management:** Handling the human and material resources and ensuring clear and effective communication across stakeholders.
- **Risk Management:** Identifying, assessing, and mitigating potential project risks.
- **Procurement and Stakeholder Management:** Managing vendors and ensuring stakeholders are engaged and informed.

3. The Balance of Theory and Practice:

PMP isn't just about knowing theoretical concepts. The certification demands both:

- **Educational Background:** Depending on one's academic background, specific hours of project management education are required.
- **Practical Experience:** Professionals need to demonstrate significant hours of leading and directing projects. This ensures that a PMP holder isn't just book-smart but has tangible, hands-on experience.

4. Rigorous Examination Process:

The PMP examination itself is a test of endurance, analytical ability, and in-depth knowledge. With 200 multiple-choice questions to be answered in four hours, it not only evaluates theoretical knowledge but also situational judgment, problem-solving abilities, and practical application of project management principles.

5. Commitment to Ethical Practices:

PMP-certified professionals are bound by the PMI Code of Ethics and Professional Conduct. This ensures they operate with integrity, fairness, honesty, and professionalism, making them trusted partners in any project.

6. Continuous Learning and PDUs:

Achieving PMP is not the end but the beginning of a continuous learning journey. To maintain their certification, professionals must earn Professional Development Units (PDUs) by engaging in training, workshops, and other relevant activities. This ensures that their knowledge remains current and relevant.

7. Career and Financial Implications:

Numerous surveys and studies have shown that PMP-certified professionals often command higher salaries compared to their non-certified counterparts. Additionally, the certification can be a significant differentiator in job applications, promotions, and project assignments.

The PMP certification, in essence, is a synthesis of rigorous training, practical experience, and a commitment to excellence. It equips professionals not just with the knowledge, but with the mindset, ethos, and global perspective needed to lead projects successfully, irrespective of scale or complexity. As the world of projects grows ever more complex and global, the PMP remains a beacon of excellence, assuring stakeholders of a professional's unmatched competence in the realm of project management.

Architecting Success for the PMP Exam: A Detailed Blueprint

In the realm of professional certifications, the Project Management Professional (PMP) exam stands out not just for its prestige but also its challenging nature. Successfully navigating this exam requires a comprehensive, well-planned approach that extends beyond rote memorization. Let's explore this blueprint of success:

1. The PMP Landscape:

Understanding the contours of the exam is the first step. The PMP exam evaluates the candidate's knowledge across several domains, such as initiating, planning, executing, monitoring and controlling, and closing projects. Moreover, it integrates the practical and theoretical elements of project management, examining one's grasp over both the art and science of this profession.

2. Building a Solid Foundation:

The PMP exam doesn't test memorization; it tests understanding. Hence, investing time in:

- **Core Concepts:** Grasp the fundamental principles of project management. Understand key terminologies, processes, and methodologies.
- **The PMBOK® Guide:** The Project Management Body of Knowledge (PMBOK® Guide) by PMI is an invaluable resource, providing a deep dive into standardized project management knowledge and practices.

3. The Role of Practical Experience:

While the PMP exam is rooted in the PMBOK® Guide, questions are often scenario-based, evaluating one's ability to apply knowledge in real-world contexts. Thus:

- **Hands-on Experience:** Engage in active project management roles, applying the principles and methodologies you've learned.
- **Case Studies:** Analyze various project management case studies. This not only enriches understanding but also provides insights into how principles are applied under different circumstances.

4. Structured Learning and Training:

There are numerous PMP prep courses available, both online and offline:

- **Select Wisely:** Opt for a course aligned with the latest version of the PMBOK® Guide. Ensure the trainers are PMP-certified professionals with substantial real-world experience.

- **Interactive Learning:** Engage in group discussions, workshops, and simulations. The more you discuss and debate, the clearer the concepts become.

5. Simulation and Mock Tests:
Regular testing is pivotal to gauge one's preparedness:

- **Practice Exams:** Take full-length mock tests to simulate the actual exam experience. This helps in time management and identifies areas needing further study.
- **Feedback Loop:** Analyze your performance. Understand the mistakes, revisit those topics, and ensure the concepts are clear.

6. Continuous Revision and Update:
The field of project management is dynamic. Keeping updated with the latest trends, tools, and methodologies is crucial. Even while preparing, keep an eye on industry news, PMI updates, and other resources.

7. Psychological and Physical Readiness:
Success in the PMP exam isn't just about intellectual preparation:

- **Stress Management:** The rigorous nature of the exam can be daunting. Engage in relaxation techniques, meditation, or any activity that helps you de-stress.
- **Physical Health:** A well-rested, healthy body complements a sharp mind. Ensure a balanced diet, regular exercise, and adequate sleep, especially as the exam date approaches.

8. The Final Leap:
On the exam day, arrive early to familiarize yourself with the environment. Stay calm, read each question carefully, and trust your preparation.

Architecting success for the PMP exam is a blend of structured learning, practical exposure, continuous revision, and mental preparedness. Like any architectural marvel, a successful PMP journey is built brick by brick, with each element carefully chosen and placed to support the overarching structure.

Why you need the PMP

The Project Management Professional (PMP) certification is not just another line to add to your resume. In the ever-evolving landscape of global business and technology, the PMP stands as a beacon of excellence, vouching for an individual's expertise, professionalism, and dedication to the discipline of project management. Here are the compelling reasons why earning this prestigious credential can be a transformative step in your career:

1. **Universal Language of Competence:** The PMP communicates universally acknowledged standards of project management. Regardless of where you are or which industry you belong to, this certification denotes a standardized level of expertise.

2. **Resilience in Volatile Job Markets:** In uncertain economic climates, a PMP certification can be a safeguard. It suggests adaptability, strategic thinking, and a commitment to excellence – traits which employers value, especially during challenging times.

3. **Broadened Horizons:** The PMP is not just about managing tasks and timelines. It delves into stakeholder management, change management, and strategic alignment, which equips professionals with a comprehensive toolkit for diverse challenges.

4. **Invaluable Peer Connections:** As a PMP holder, you gain access to a global community of

experts. These networks can lead to collaborative opportunities, mentorship, and even new career paths.

5. **Credibility Boost:** The PMP is a seal of approval, indicating that the holder has met stringent testing and experiential requirements. This instantly amplifies professional credibility.

6. **Adaptability in the Digital Age:** In our rapidly digitizing world, the ability to manage complex digital projects is invaluable. The PMP curriculum is continuously updated, ensuring that its holders are always ahead of the curve in digital project management trends.

7. **Bolstered Negotiation Abilities:** One overlooked aspect of project management is the art of negotiation, whether it's resource allocation, scope changes, or stakeholder expectations. The PMP curriculum equips professionals with the nuanced skills required for these delicate interactions.

8. **Catalyst for Continuous Improvement:** Achieving the PMP is not the end but a beginning. It instills a mindset of ongoing growth and learning, essential in

our rapidly evolving professional landscape.

9. **Benchmark for Excellence:** Organizations increasingly use the PMP as a benchmark when considering promotions, role allocations, or new hires. It's becoming a standard for excellence in several industries.

10. **Upholder of Integrity:** Beyond the technicalities, PMP-certified professionals are trained to approach projects ethically. This means making decisions that are not just effective but also morally sound, enhancing trust with stakeholders and clients.

To encapsulate, the PMP isn't merely a certification; it's a philosophy. It encompasses a wide spectrum of skills, from strategic planning to ethical decision-making, making its holders invaluable assets in any professional arena.

How to Prepare for the PMP

The PMP (Project Management Professional) certification, offered by the Project Management Institute (PMI), is a globally recognized and sought-after credential in the field of project management. Preparing for the PMP examination requires strategic planning, commitment, and a combination of theoretical study and practical understanding. Here are comprehensive steps, gleaned from 30 years of educational experience, to guide you toward exam success:

1. Understand the PMP Exam Requirements:

Before you embark on your study journey, ensure you meet the prerequisites:

- **Educational Background**: A secondary degree (high school diploma, associate's degree, or global equivalent) or a four-year degree.
- **Project Management Experience**: Depending on your educational background, the hours will vary. With a four-year degree, you'd typically need 3 years (or 4,500 hours) of project management experience; with a secondary degree, it's usually 5 years (or 7,500 hours).
- **Project Management Education**: 35 contact hours of formal education.

2. Familiarize Yourself with the Exam Content:

The examination is grounded in the PMI's **A Guide to the Project Management Body of Knowledge (PMBOK® Guide)**. Ensure you're well-acquainted with its structure, processes, and knowledge areas.

3. Design a Study Plan:

A well-structured plan is key:

- **Duration**: Aim for a 2-4 month study window. Adjust based on your availability.
- **Resources**: Besides the PMBOK® Guide, invest in reputable PMP prep books, online courses, and simulation exams.
- **Consistency**: Dedicate specific hours daily. Whether its early mornings or late evenings, find your peak concentration time.
- **Breaks**: Every hour, take a 10-minute break. It aids retention and reduces burnout.

4. Engage in Active Learning:

- **Flashcards**: Create or purchase flashcards to reinforce key terms, processes, and concepts.
- **Practice Questions**: Answering mock questions

daily hones your test-taking skills.

- **Discussion Groups**: Join online forums or local PMP study groups. Engaging in discussions deepens comprehension.

5. Simulated Exams:

Allocate time for at least 3-4 full-length simulation exams. These tests:

- Gauge your readiness.
- Familiarize you with the exam format.
- Improve time management during the actual exam.

6. Review and Refine:

After each simulation exam, review your mistakes. Understand why you chose an incorrect answer. Strengthen weak areas with focused study.

7. Real-World Application:

Connect theoretical knowledge with practical experience. Reflect on past projects and understand how PMBOK® concepts were applied, or could have been implemented more effectively.

8. Maintain Your Well-being:

Physical health, mental well-being, and nutrition play a role in your preparation. Regular exercise, adequate sleep, and a balanced diet boost cognitive functions and concentration.

9. Final Review:

In the last week before your exam, review your notes, and focus on key areas, formulas, and processes. However, avoid cramming; it's counterproductive.

10. Exam Day Tips:

- **Stay Calm**: Anxiety can hinder performance. Practice deep breathing if you feel overwhelmed.
- **Time Management**: Don't spend too much time on one question. Mark it and move on. Return to it later if needed.
- **Breaks**: Utilize the allowed breaks during the exam. A few minutes of stretching and relaxation can refocus the mind.

In conclusion, preparing for the PMP exam requires a blend of structured study, real-world application, and self-care. With dedication, persistence, and the right strategies, acing the PMP exam is within your reach. Remember, it's not just about passing the exam but truly understanding and internalizing the knowledge and skills that will elevate your project management career.

Improve your chances of Obtaining the PMP

The journey towards acquiring the Project Management Professional (PMP) certification is challenging, yet deeply rewarding. This globally recognized credential signifies a project manager's competency, commitment, and capability. Over the course of my 30 years in education, I have observed the transformation that comes with such professional qualifications. Allow me to share some wisdom on how you can enhance your odds of success.

1. **Deep Understanding of PMBOK® Guide**: The Project Management Body of Knowledge (PMBOK® Guide) serves as a cornerstone for PMP exams. Dive deep into its content, understand the processes, and familiarize yourself with the terminology. A surface-level reading will not suffice. Instead, consider the guide as your Bible for the exam and study it multiple times.

2. **Apply Real-world Scenarios**: It's essential not only to know the theory but also to understand its application. Relate every principle, process, and tool to real-world projects you've encountered. If you haven't personally experienced them, seek out case studies or examples. This strategy aids in cementing knowledge and offers a practical perspective during the exam.

3. **Practice Makes Perfect**: Just like any significant exam, practice is vital. Solve as many mock tests as you can. These tests not only familiarize you with the question format but also help you manage your time better. They highlight your strengths and pinpoint areas that require more focus.

4. **Form Study Groups**: Collaborative learning often aids in understanding complex topics. Join or form study groups. Discussing topics, quizzing each other, or explaining concepts aloud to a group can reinforce your understanding and unveil different perspectives.

5. **Stay Updated on Exam Changes**: PMI regularly revises the PMP exam to stay current with the evolving world of project management. Ensure you are preparing from the most recent edition of study materials and are aware of

any changes in the exam format or content.

6. **Diversify Your Study Resources**: Don't limit yourself to just one book or source. There are numerous supplementary materials, online forums, webinars, and courses available. Diversifying your resources exposes you to various teaching methodologies and provides a comprehensive view of topics.

7. **Mindset and Attitude**: Your psychological state plays a pivotal role. Approach the exam with a positive attitude and confidence, but not overconfidence. Regular breaks, physical exercise, and relaxation techniques can aid in reducing stress and enhancing focus.

8. **Pacing and Strategy**: The PMP exam isn't just about what you know; it's also about how you approach the questions. Develop a strategy for the exam day. Decide on how much time you'll spend on each question, when you'll review answers, and what type of questions to tackle first. This strategy will prevent you from feeling overwhelmed and help you manage the allocated time efficiently.

9. **Continuous Feedback Loop**: After every mock test or study session, evaluate your performance. Understand where you went wrong, revisit those topics, and rectify your mistakes. This iterative learning process is essential for continuous improvement.

10. **Stay Committed**: Remember, the journey is demanding, but perseverance is key. Set a regular study schedule, stick to it, and avoid procrastination. Surround yourself with motivational triggers, be it success stories or supportive peers.

In conclusion, obtaining the PMP certification is a testament to your expertise and dedication in the field of project management. The preparation journey, while rigorous, is an invaluable learning experience in itself. With determination, the right strategies, and resources, you can certainly enhance your chances of wearing the prestigious PMP badge with pride.

The PMP Application Audit Process

The application process for the PMP certification is quite rigorous to ensure that only qualified professionals earn the credential. One aspect of this application process is the potential for an application audit.

The PMP Application Audit Process:

- **Purpose of the Audit**:
    - The primary objective of the PMP application audit is to maintain the integrity and credibility of the PMP certification program by validating the applicant's experience, education, and professional qualifications. It's a way for PMI (Project Management Institute) to ensure that the information provided by candidates is accurate and verifiable.
- **Selection for Audit**:
    - Not all PMP applications are audited. Instead, a certain percentage are selected at random after the payment for the PMP examination is made. It's also worth noting that you won't know if you've been selected for an audit until after you've submitted your application and made the payment.
- **Required Documentation**:
    - If your application is selected for an audit, you'll be asked to provide supporting documentation for the information you've presented. This can include:
- **Proof of Education**: A copy of your diploma or degree.
- **Proof of Project Management Education**: Certificates from the training institutes or course providers verifying the 35 contact hours of formal education you've claimed.
- **Experience Verification**: Signed declarations from your supervisor or managers for the projects you've listed in your application. This will verify your role, responsibilities, and duration of the project.

- **Timeframe for Compliance**:
  - Typically, once notified of the audit, you have 90 days to gather and submit the required documentation.
- **Submitting the Documentation**:
  - All audit documents should be sent in one envelope to expedite the processing time. It's advisable to use a traceable method of shipping to ensure the documents are received by PMI.
- **Post Submission**:
  - Once PMI receives your audit materials, they will generally process them within 5-7 business days. If your documentation meets the criteria and everything is verified, PMI will send you an eligibility code, which you can use to schedule your examination.
- **In Case of Audit Failure**:
  - If there's any discrepancy in the documentation or if you fail to meet the audit requirements, PMI might decline your eligibility to take the PMP exam. It's essential to be accurate and honest in your application to avoid this situation.

Tips for a Smooth Audit Process:
1. **Be Prepared**: Even if you aren't selected for an audit, it's a good idea to have all your supporting documentation ready when you fill out the PMP application. This way, if you are audited, you're prepared.
2. **Accuracy is Key**: Ensure that all information, especially your project management experience, is described accurately on your application. Any exaggeration or misinformation can result in failure during the audit.
3. **Maintain Communication**: Stay in touch with your references, as PMI might contact them for verification. Inform them in advance so they are aware and can provide a timely response.

Ensuring Success in the PMP Audit:

8. **Detailed Project Descriptions**:
   - When describing your project experiences, provide detailed descriptions, but avoid jargon. Clearly explain your role in each project, the methodologies used, and your specific contributions. PMI wants to understand your firsthand experience in project management roles.

9. **Consistency is Vital**:
   - Ensure that the dates, roles, and other details on your application align with what your references will confirm. Inconsistencies, even if unintentional, can raise flags during the audit.

10. **Relevant Contact Details**:
    - Provide updated and accurate contact information for all your references. Should PMI need to verify any detail, this step ensures a swift process without unnecessary delays.

11. **Record Keeping**:
    - For your benefit, maintain a personal file of all the projects you've worked on, including project duration, description, key deliverables, and your role. This not only aids in filling out the PMP application but also becomes invaluable during the audit.

12. **Professional Conduct**:
    - Remember that the audit process isn't a test but a verification. Approach it professionally. If there are any hiccups or if PMI asks for additional information, be prompt and respectful in your responses.

13. **Possible Reapplication**:
    - If, for any reason, the audit doesn't go well, it's not the end of your PMP journey.

Understand the feedback, address the discrepancies, gain more experience if needed, and reapply. Many professionals face challenges in their first application but succeed in subsequent attempts.

your PMP journey can be both enlightening and rewarding.

Wrapping Up:

While the PMP application audit process may seem daunting, remember that it exists to uphold the standard of the PMP certification and ensure only qualified individuals earn the title. By understanding the process and being proactive, you can make the audit phase a straightforward one.

It's also beneficial to be part of local PMI chapters or online forums where PMP aspirants and certified professionals share their experiences. This peer-learning can provide invaluable insights and practical tips on navigating the audit process.

Finally, embrace the process. Earning the PMP certification is a significant achievement, and every step, including the audit, brings you closer to joining the ranks of elite project management professionals worldwide. With dedication, honesty, and the right preparation,

Chapter Two: How to Ace the Examination

*A*chieving mastery in the PMP exam is a journey that demands dedication, strategic planning, and effective resources. Here's an expanded guide:

1. **Understand the Exam Format and Structure:** The PMP exam comprises 180 questions of varying formats. For instance, multiple-choice questions might ask you to pick the best answer from four options, while hotspot questions might ask you to pinpoint an area on an image. Familiarize yourself with each question type by accessing sample questions from the PMI website or trusted PMP resources.

2. **Use the PMBOK Guide:** The PMBOK Guide is your foundational text. It's like the textbook for a course. For practicality, take notes in the margins, highlight key areas, and create summaries for each chapter. For instance, the guide might elaborate on 'Earned Value Management'. Understand the formula, its application, and then maybe illustrate it with an example from a personal or hypothetical project.

3. **Enroll in a PMP Prep Course:** While self-study has its merits, prep courses offer structured learning. For example, a session might be dedicated to 'Risk Management'. The instructor might share real-world scenarios, making complex concepts relatable. Always research course reviews and get recommendations before enrolling.

4. **Establish a Study Schedule:** Instead of a vague "study every day" plan, be specific. For instance, "Monday - 2 hours post-dinner dedicated to 'Project Integration Management'". Setting such precise targets helps in tracking progress and maintaining discipline.

5. **Practice with Mock Exams:** Mock exams aren't just about answering questions; they're about simulating the exam environment. Find a quiet spot, time yourself,

and attempt the exam without interruptions. After completing, analyze your mistakes. For example, if you consistently get 'Quality Management' questions wrong, you know where to focus.

6. **Engage in Study Groups:** Think of these groups as mini brainstorming sessions. For instance, if you're struggling with 'Stakeholder Management', someone else might offer a unique strategy or mnemonic that helps. Online forums, such as Reddit or dedicated PMP forums, can also be a good platform.

7. **Focus on Quality, Not Quantity:** Instead of reading the same chapter thrice, read it once but with focus. Relate concepts to real-world applications. For instance, when understanding 'Scope Creep', recall a project where unplanned changes affected the outcome.

8. **Review Regularly:** Use tools like flashcards. For example, one side of the card might have 'PERT Analysis', and the flip side could detail its formula and application.

Regularly shuffling and testing yourself with these cards can reinforce memory.

9. **Mind Your Health:** The brain functions best when well-rested and nourished. For instance, foods rich in Omega-3, like fish or walnuts, are known to boost cognitive functions. And remember, hydration is key.

10. **Stay Updated:** Project management, like all fields, evolves. Subscribe to PMI newsletters or join a PMP community. Any recent shifts or updates can be crucial for your preparation.

11. **Develop Test-Taking Strategies:** For example, if a question confuses you, mark it and move on. Sometimes, subsequent questions can provide context or jog your memory. Also, for questions you're unsure about, use the process of elimination. Removing obviously incorrect answers can increase your chances of choosing the right one.

12. **Day before the Exam:** Think of it as a marathon day. Athletes don't run

extensively the day before; they rest and carb-load. Similarly, avoid cramming. Set your documents, IDs, and essentials in a bag, so there's no rush on the exam day.

13. **On Exam Day:** A calm mind can think clearer. Use deep breathing techniques if you feel anxious. Remember, every question has an answer, and you've prepared for them all. Trust your preparation.

In essence, preparing for the PMP exam is a mix of structured learning, practice, and self-care. Commit to the journey, and the destination of success will be well within reach.

Tips and Tricks

1. **Understanding, Not Memorization:**
PMP is about understanding the principles and processes of project management. Avoid rote memorization. Instead, focus on truly understanding the concepts. This understanding will enable you to answer scenario-based questions, which test the application of knowledge.

2. **Know the PMBOK Guide:**
The PMBOK (Project Management Body of Knowledge) Guide is the primary reference for the exam. Familiarize yourself with its structure, its processes, and the key terminologies. However, understand that the exam is not limited to PMBOK. It tests real-world application and understanding beyond the guide.

3. **Practice with Mock Tests:**
Experience has shown that students who take multiple mock tests tend to perform better. These tests familiarize you with the exam pattern, improve time management skills, and help you identify areas for improvement.

4. **Active Learning Techniques:**
Engage in active learning methods such as teaching what you've learned to someone else, discussing topics in study groups, or even making flashcards. These techniques can be particularly beneficial for understanding complex topics.

5. **Mind Maps and Visual Aids:**
Many of the processes and methodologies in PMP can be better understood using visual aids. Creating mind maps can help you visualize interrelationships and overlapping areas between different knowledge domains.

6. **Breaks are Essential:**
Your brain can only focus for so long before it needs a short break. Studies have shown that taking regular breaks can enhance overall retention and understanding. Use

techniques like the Pomodoro Technique where you study for 25 minutes and then take a 5-minute break.

7. Real-World Application:

Try to relate the concepts to real-world scenarios or projects you've worked on. This not only reinforces the concepts but also gives you practical examples you can draw upon when answering scenario-based questions.

8. Focus on ITTOs (Inputs, Tools, Techniques, and Outputs):

Understanding ITTOs is crucial. However, don't just memorize them; try to understand the logic and reasoning behind each one.

9. Stay Updated:

The world of project management is always evolving, and so is the PMP exam. Ensure you are studying the latest material and are aware of any changes or updates to the PMBOK and the PMP exam content.

10. Health and Well-being:

Last but not least, take care of your physical and mental well-being. A balanced diet, regular exercise, and adequate sleep play a significant role in your ability to study effectively and perform well on the exam.

What to do before the Exam

1. **Understanding the PMP Exam Content Outline**: Before you start any kind of preparation, familiarize yourself with the PMP Exam Content Outline. This document, provided by PMI, details the domains and tasks associated with the roles of a project manager. Knowing what's on the test ensures you cover all bases.

2. **Establish a Study Routine**:

- **Routine Setting**: Consistency is key. Decide on a fixed number of hours per day or week and stick to it. Remember, it's better to study for an hour every day than to cram for seven hours in one day.

- **Study Environment**: Choose a quiet, well-lit place. Ensure minimal distractions. This helps improve focus and retention.

3. **Gather High-Quality Resources**:

- **PMBOK Guide**: This is the primary reference book for PMP exam preparation. It's essential to have the most recent edition.

- **Complementary Books**: While PMBOK is indispensable, consider supplemental materials like Rita Mulcahy's PMP Exam Prep or Andy Crowe's book. They offer different perspectives, examples, and practice questions.

- **Online Resources**: Websites, forums, and online courses can be beneficial. Sites like PMI's official website, Project Management PrepCast, and others offer exam simulations, webinars, and practice questions.

4. **Join a Study Group**:

- Engage with peers preparing for the PMP. A study group allows you to view concepts from different perspectives, clarify doubts, and stay motivated.

5. **Practice Makes Perfect**:

- **Simulated Exams**: Take as many full-length simulated exams as possible. They give you a taste of the real exam and help with time management.

- **Review Mistakes**: It's not just about taking tests. Review your mistakes and understand the concepts behind the questions you got wrong. This iterative learning will build strong foundations.

6. **Focus on Key Areas**:

- **Formulas**: Be proficient with PMP formulas, especially those related to cost management, time value of money, and earned value management.

- **ITTOs (Inputs, Tools, Techniques, and Outputs)**: While it's impractical to memorize all ITTOs, understand their logic and flow. This will make it easier to tackle questions that revolve around them.

7. **Take Care of Yourself**:

- **Rest and Sleep**: Do not underestimate the power of a good night's sleep, especially in the days leading up to the exam.

- **Diet**: Maintain a balanced diet. Omega-3s and antioxidants, found in fish, nuts, and berries, can boost brain power.

- **Exercise**: Physical activity can enhance cognition and alleviate stress.

8. **Review PMI's Exam Policies and Procedures**:

- Familiarize yourself with the exam format, question types, and policies. Knowing what to expect will minimize surprises on the test day.

9. **Test Center and Logistics**:

- Scout the exam location in advance. Know the parking situation, public transport options, and building location.

- Understand the procedures for the exam day – the kind of ID required, items allowed in the examination room, etc.

10. **Mindset**:

- **Positive Attitude**: Remember that preparation is key. Be confident in your abilities and the effort you've put in.

- **Stress Management**: Engage in deep-breathing exercises, meditation, or any other activity that relaxes your mind. Keeping calm will improve performance.

What to do on the Exam Day

1. **Rest and Relaxation the Night Before:** Begin your preparations the evening prior. Ensure you have a restful night's sleep. Resist the urge to cram. Your brain requires adequate rest to function at its peak.

2. **Nutrition and Hydration:** Eat a balanced breakfast. You don't want hunger to distract you during the exam. Avoid excessive caffeine as it might increase anxiety. Drink enough water but not too much to avoid frequent bathroom breaks.

3. **Dress Comfortably:** Wear comfortable, layered clothing. Examination rooms can vary in temperature, and you'll want to be prepared to adjust accordingly.

4. **Pack Essentials the Night Before:** Prepare your identification, exam confirmation, any required documentation, and

essentials in one place. This reduces morning stress.

5. **Arrive Early:** Reach the exam center at least 30 minutes before your scheduled time. This allows for any unexpected issues, such as traffic, and gives you a buffer to mentally prepare.

6. **Mindset Matters:** Approach the exam with a positive attitude. Remember, you've prepared thoroughly. Take deep breaths and remain calm. Visualization techniques, such as imagining a successful exam experience, can also set a positive tone.

7. **Understand the Exam Format:** Before you start, familiarize yourself with the structure of the exam, the time limit, and any provided resources like a calculator or reference sheet.

8. **Time Management:** Monitor your pace. While you don't want to rush, be aware of the time. If you encounter a challenging question, mark it and move on. You can return to it later.

9. **Read Questions Carefully:** Misinterpretation can lead to wrong answers. Ensure you understand what's being asked. Look out for keywords and phrases, and don't make assumptions.

10. **Trust Your Preparation:** You've spent considerable time preparing. When in doubt, rely on your foundational knowledge and best judgment. It's okay to trust your first instinct on answers.

11. **Take Breaks, if allowed:** If the format permits, take short breaks to stretch and breathe. This can help refresh your mind.

12. **Review, but Not Obsessively:** If time allows, revisit marked questions. However, don't second-guess every answer. Often, your initial instinct is correct.

13. **Once Finished:** After completing the exam, take a moment to ensure you haven't missed any questions. Once you're satisfied, submit your exam.

14. **Post-Exam Decompression:** Regardless of how you feel

post-exam, take some time for yourself. Engage in a relaxing activity or treat yourself. Remember, the exam is just one step in your professional journey.

Tips for Answering Questions

1. **Understand the Question Structure:** PMP questions are designed to test your understanding, application, and analysis skills related to the project management processes. Before attempting to answer, ensure you grasp the essence of the question.

2. **Elimination Technique:** There are often one or two options that are clearly incorrect. Begin by eliminating them. This narrows down your choices and increases your chances of selecting the correct answer.

3. **Choose the Best Answer:** PMP might present multiple answers that seem correct. However, your goal is to pick the 'best' one. This often requires applying PMI's perspective, even if it conflicts with your real-world experience.

4. **Read All Options:** Before settling on an answer, read all the available options. Sometimes, the last option is the most appropriate one.

5. **Pace Yourself:** It's crucial to maintain a steady pace. While you shouldn't rush, you also don't want to spend too much time on a single challenging question. If you're unsure, mark it and come back to it later.

6. **Use Visual Aids:** For questions involving data or processes, sketching a quick chart or diagram might help visualize and better understand the information.

7. **Rely on Your Training:** The PMP exam is rooted in the PMBOK® Guide and other PMI resources. Always revert to the fundamentals you've learned during your preparation.

8. **Beware of Absolute Terms:** Words like "always," "never," "must," or "only" are red flags. In the complex realm of project management, few things are absolute.

9. **Stay Calm and Positive:** Anxiety can cloud judgment. Take deep breaths if you feel nervous, and maintain a positive attitude. Believe in your preparation.

10. **Context is Key:** Consider the context in which the question is framed. Is it during the initiating phase? Closing? Your answer might vary based on the phase of the project.

11. **Use Exam Strategies:** If you come across a difficult question, try to answer it from a theoretical standpoint rather than how you would handle it in a real-life scenario. The PMP exam tests knowledge according to PMI standards, which may not always align with real-world practices.

12. **Review before Submitting:** If time allows, revisit the questions you've marked or were uncertain about. Don't change answers unless you're sure; often, your first instinct is correct.

13. **Stay Updated:** PMI occasionally updates the PMP exam to reflect changes in the profession. Ensure you're preparing using the most recent materials and are aware of any changes in the examination content.

14. **Remember Ethical Considerations:** Many questions may touch on the PMI Code of Ethics and Professional Conduct. When in doubt, choose the answer that best aligns with ethical standards.

15. **Practice Regularly:** Before the actual exam, take as many mock tests as you can. This will not only familiarize you with the format but also build your confidence and time-management skills.

Exam Overview

Behind every certification exam, you can be sure to find exam objectives—the broad topics in which the exam developers want to ensure your competency. PMP ® exam objectives are listed below;

Building foundation

- Be able to describe the difference between projects and operations. A project is temporary in nature with a definite beginning and ending date. Projects produce unique products, services, or results. Operations are ongoing and use repetitive processes that typically produce the same result over and over.
- Be able to distinguish between the seven needs or demands that bring about project creation. The seven needs or demands that bring about project creation are market demand, organizational need, customer requests, technological advances, legal requirements, ecological impacts, and social needs.
- Be able to describe a feasibility study. A feasibility study is used to determine the viability of the project, the probability of success, and the viability of the product, service, or result of the project.
- Be able to name the five project management process groups. The five project management process groups are Initiating, Planning, Executing, Monitoring and Controlling, and Closing.
- Be able to denote the skills listed in the PMI® Talent Triangle™. The three skills are technical project management, leadership, and strategic and business management. Be able to denote some of the skills every good project manager should possess. Communication, organizational, problem solving, negotiation and influencing, leading, team building, technical, and business knowledge are skills a project manager should possess.
- Be able to name the three types of PMO organizations. The three types of PMO organizations are supportive, controlling, and directive.
- Be able to name the three types of development life cycles. They are predictive (known as waterfall),

adaptive (known as agile), and hybrid.

- Be able to describe the agile project management methodology. A method of managing projects in small, incremental portions of work that can be easily assigned, easily managed, and completed within a short period of time. Agile involves continuous stakeholder involvement and feedback.
- Be able to describe the difference between Scrum and Kanban. Scrum and Kanban are both agile methodologies. Scrum teams complete work in short, time-bound periods called sprints. Kanban is a continuous system. The work does not start and stop but continues through to completion. Kanban is also known as an on-demand scheduling system. Both Scrum and Kanban are known as pull systems.

Assessing project needs
- Be able to name the 10 Project Management Knowledge Areas. The 10 Project Management Knowledge Areas are Project Integration Management, Project Scope Management, Project

Schedule Management, Project Cost Management, Project Quality Management, Project Resource Management, Project Communications Management, Project Risk Management, Project Procurement Management, and Project Stakeholder Management.
- Be able to define project selection methods. Project selection methods are used prior to the Develop Project Charter process to determine the viability of the project. The most common are the benefit measurement methods, which include comparative approaches and cash flow analysis.
- Be able to describe and calculate the payback period. The payback period is the amount of time it will take the company to recoup its initial investment in the product of the project. It's calculated by adding up the expected cash inflows and comparing them to the initial investment to determine how many periods it takes for the cash inflows to equal the initial investment.
- Be able to denote the decision criteria for NPV and

IRR. Projects with an NPV greater than 0 should be accepted, and those with an NPV less than 0 should be rejected. Projects with high IRR values should be accepted over projects with lower IRR values. IRR is the discount rate when NPV is equal to 0, and IRR assumes reinvestment at the IRR rate.

- Be able to describe tailoring. Tailoring means determining the documents and project process needed for the project when considering the size and complexity of the project. This also involves keeping the project artifacts (such as the business case, benefits management plan, project charter, and the project management plan) coordinated and aligned with one another and with the organization's strategic goals.

- Be able to describe integration. Integration involves repeating processes continuously while you're working on the project and coordinating all aspects of the project management plan. Integration is highly interactive. According to the PMBOK® Guide, performing integration is a critical skill that all project managers should possess.

- Be able to explain integration when using an agile methodology. Integration is managed and performed by the project manager when using an agile project management methodology, and the planning, control, and delivery of the product is managed by the agile team.

- Be able to describe the purpose of the business case. The purpose of a business case is to understand the business need for the project and determine whether the investment in the project is worthwhile. It is considered an economic feasibility study. It usually includes a benefit–cost ratio analysis and the needs or demands that brought about the project. This is an input to the Develop Project Charter process.

- Be able to describe the purpose of the benefits management plan. The benefits management plan outlines the intended benefit of the project, how those benefits will be measured, and how they will be obtained. Owners are assigned to each benefit to ensure they are achieved. The benefits management plan is monitored throughout the life of the project. This is an input to the Develop Project Charter process.

- Be able to describe the importance of the project charter. The approved project charter is the document that officially recognizes and acknowledges that a project exists. The charter authorizes the project to begin, authorizes the project manager to assign resources to the project, documents the business need and justification, describes the customer's requirements, and ties the project to the ongoing work of the organization.

Delivering Business Value
- Be able to differentiate the organizational structures and the project manager's authority in each. Organizations are usually structured in some combination of the following: functional, project-oriented, and matrix (including weak matrix, balanced matrix, and strong matrix). Project managers have the most authority in a project-oriented organization and the least amount of authority in a functional organization.

- Understand the Identify Stakeholders process. The purpose of this process is to identify the project stakeholders, assess their influence and level of involvement, and record stakeholder information in the stakeholder register.

- Understand stakeholder analysis. Stakeholder analysis is performed using qualitative and quantitative data. Some of the tools and techniques used to accomplish this are expert judgment, data gathering, data analysis, data representation, and meetings.

- Understand the ways to categorize and display stakeholder analysis. Categorizing and displaying stakeholder analysis can take several forms including: power/interest grid, power/influence grid, impact/influence grid, stakeholder cube, the Salience model, directions of influence, and prioritization.

- Be able to name the categories, qualitative

classes, and subclasses of the Salience model. The categories are power, legitimacy, and urgency. The qualitative classes are latent, expectant, and demanding. The subclasses within latent are dormant, discretionary, and demanding. The subclasses within expectant are dominant, dependent, and dangerous. Demanding stakeholders have the attributes of all three categories: power, legitimacy, and urgency.

- Be able to name the key components of the stakeholder register. One component is the identifying information such as name, title, and contact information. Another component is assessment information, including needs and interests. Last is stakeholder classification, in terms of power and influence.

- Be able to name the key roles on a Scrum team. The key roles are the product owner (also known as the voice of the customer), the Scrum team (these are the team members who make up the team), and the Scrum master and/or team facilitator.

- Be able to describe business value and examine this throughout the project. Business value refers to those values that will lead to short- and long-term benefits for the organization. The project manager should champion the business value vision and examine and measure business value throughout the project.

- Understand the opportunities to deliver value incrementally. It is the responsibility of the project manager to deliver business value. The project manager should help the team define the opportunities to deliver value incrementally.

- Support the team to subdivide tasks and find the minimum viable product. The minimum viable product involves breaking down tasks into tangible components that have enough features and functionality to allow the customer to examine value and provide feedback to the team.

Developing Project Scope
- Be able to state the purpose of the Develop Project Management Plan process. It defines, coordinates, and

integrates all subsidiary project plans.

- Be able to describe the purpose of the scope management plan. The scope management plan has a direct influence on the project's success and describes the process for determining project scope, facilitates creating the WBS, describes how the product or service of the project is validated and accepted, and documents how changes to scope will be handled. The scope management plan is a subsidiary plan of the project management plan. The scope management plan defines, maintains, and manages the scope of the project.
- Understand the purpose of the project scope management plan and requirements management plan. The scope management plan and requirements management plan help set a clear vision and mission for the project and are used to plan and manage the scope of the project.
- Understand the purpose of the project scope statement. The project scope statement serves as an agreement between the project management team and the project customer that states precisely what the work of the project will produce. The project objectives and deliverables and their quantifiable criteria are documented in the scope statement and are used by the project manager and the stakeholders to determine whether the project was completed successfully. It also serves as a basis for future project decisions.
- Be able to describe the product backlog. The product backlog is a list of all the user stories (deliverables and requirements) that are needed to complete the project. You'll document the user stories at the beginning of the project, before the work starts, and then compile them in the product backlog.
- Be able to describe the backlog. The backlog consists of the user stories that will be worked on during the iteration. The agile team breaks down the user stories into tasks, and each team member chooses the tasks they want to work on during the iteration.

- Be able to define project constraints and assumptions. Project constraints limit the options of the project team and restrict their actions. Sometimes constraints dictate actions. Time, budget, and scope are the most common constraints. Assumptions are conditions that are presumed to be true or real. They are both documented in the assumption log. Be able to define a WBS and its components. The WBS is a deliverable-oriented hierarchy. It uses the deliverables from the project scope statement or similar documents and decomposes them into logical, manageable units of work. The first level of decomposition is the major deliverable level or subproject level, the second level of decomposition is a further elaboration of the deliverables, and so on. The lowest level of any WBS is called a work package. User stories are the work package level for an agile or hybrid project.
- Understand the difference between code of accounts identifiers and control accounts. Code of accounts identifiers are assigned to all elements of a WBS. These are a unique numbering system that ties the work elements to the code of accounts. A control account consists of two or more work packages (each with their own code of accounts identifier) and/or one or more planning packages. A control account is inserted between a major deliverable and the work package, and it tracks cost, schedule, and scope and is also used to perform earned value measurements. A planning package is inserted between the control account and the work package level and does not include schedule activities.
- Be able to name the components of the scope baseline. The scope baseline consists of the approved project scope statement, WBS, work packages, planning packages, and the WBS dictionary.

Creating the Project Schedule

- Be able to describe the purpose of the Estimate Activity Resources process. The purpose of Estimate Activity Resources is to determine the types of resources needed (human, equipment, and materials) and in what quantities for each schedule activity within a work package.

- Be familiar with the tools and techniques of Estimate Activity Durations. The tools and techniques of Estimate Activity Durations are expert judgment, analogous estimating, parametric estimating, three-point estimating, bottom-up estimating, data analysis (alternatives analysis, reserve analysis) decision-making, and meetings.

- Know the difference between analogous estimating and bottom-up estimating. Analogous estimating is a top-down technique that uses expert judgment and historical information. Bottom-up estimating performs estimates for each work item and rolls them up to a total.

- Be able to calculate the critical path. The critical path includes the activities with durations that add up to the longest path of the project schedule network diagram. Critical path is calculated using the forward pass, backward pass, and float calculations. Be able to define a critical path task. A critical path task is a project activity with zero or negative float.

- Be able to describe and calculate PERT duration estimates. This is a weighted average technique that uses three estimates: optimistic, pessimistic, and most likely. The formula is as follows: (optimistic + pessimistic + (4 × most likely)) / 6.

- Be able to describe the difference between resource leveling and resource smoothing. Resource leveling can change the critical path and project end date. Resource smoothing does not change the critical path or project end date.

- Be familiar with the duration compression techniques. The duration compression techniques are crashing and fast tracking.

- Be able to describe a critical chain. The critical chain is the new critical path in a modified schedule that accounts for limited resources and feeding buffers.

- Know the key outputs of the Develop Schedule process. The key outputs are the project schedule and schedule baseline.

- Understand the estimating techniques for a project. Expert judgment is used most frequently on agile projects, but other techniques such as parametric estimating or bottom-up estimating will work.
- Understand how to determine activity durations for an agile project. Activity durations can be calculated using the number of iterations needed to complete the work, using the number of story points needed to complete the work, or using average velocity to determine how many story points can be completed in each iteration.
- Be able to describe a Kanban board and a Scrum board and the difference between them. Kanban boards and Scrum boards are visual displays of the work of the project. Kanban uses cards or tasks, and Scrum uses tasks. Tasks are added to the first column, usually the backlog or user story column, and then broken down into tasks and pulled into the remaining columns as the work finishes. Kanban boards and their work are capacity bound. The work is progressive and continuous.

There isn't a start and stop date. Scrum boards are time bound and display the work of the sprint.

Developing the project budget and engaging stakeholders
- Be able to state the purpose of the cost management plan. The cost management plan is the only output of the Plan Cost Management process. It establishes policies and procedures for planning and executing project costs and documents the processes for estimating, managing, and controlling project costs.
- Be able to identify and describe the primary output of the Estimate Costs process. Cost estimates are the primary output of Estimate Costs. These estimates are quantitative amounts—usually stated in monetary units—that reflect the cost of the resources needed to complete the project activities.
- Be able to identify additional general management techniques that can be used in the Project Cost Management Knowledge Area. Some of the general management

techniques that can be used in this Knowledge Area are return on investment, discounted cash flow, and payback analysis.

- Be able to describe the cost baseline. The cost baseline is the authorized, time-phased cost of the project when using budget-at completion calculations. The cost baseline is displayed as an S curve.

- Be able to describe project funding requirements. Project funding requirements are one output of the Determine Budget process. They detail the funding requirements needed on the project by time period (monthly, quarterly, annually).

- Be able to describe the purpose of the Plan Stakeholder Engagement process. The Plan Stakeholder Engagement process concerns effectively engaging stakeholders, understanding their needs and interests, identifying how they may help or hurt the project, and determining how the project will impact them. The primary output of this process is the stakeholder engagement plan.

- Be able to describe the primary purpose of the stakeholder engagement plan. The stakeholder engagement plan documents the engagement levels of the stakeholders and strategies for engaging stakeholders throughout the project.

- Be able to describe the purpose of the communications management plan. The communications management plan determines the communication needs of the stakeholders. It documents what information will be distributed, how it will be distributed, to whom, and the timing of the distribution.

- Be able to describe the difference between iterative and incremental life cycle approaches. Iterative approaches focus on discovery of the product, rather than speed of delivery. Incremental approaches deliver completed functionality at the end of the iteration that the customer can use. This increases the speed at which the team can deliver.

- Be able to name the two types of agile life cycle methodologies. Iteration-based agile involves time-bound periods of work, and flow-based agile involves work based on capacity. Be able to describe the hybrid methodology. Hybrid is a combination of methodologies, typically combining predictive approaches with agile approaches.
- Be able to name several adaptive methodologies. Examples are Extreme Programming, Crystal, Scrumban, Feature-Driven Development, Dynamic Systems Development Method, and Agile Unified Process.

Identify project risk

- Be able to define the purpose of the risk management plan. The risk management plan describes how you will define, monitor, and manage risks throughout the project. It details how risk management processes (including Identify Risks, Perform Qualitative Risk Analysis, Perform Quantitative Risk Analysis, Plan Risk Responses, Implement Risk Responses, and Monitor Risks) will be implemented, monitored, and controlled throughout the life of the project. It describes how you will manage risks but does not attempt to define responses to individual risks. The risk management plan is a subsidiary of the project management plan, and it's the only output of the Plan Risk Management process.
- Be able to name the purpose of Identify Risks. The purpose of the Identify Risks process is to identify all risks that might impact the project and then document them and identify their characteristics.
- Be able to define the purpose of Perform Qualitative Risk Analysis. Perform Qualitative Risk Analysis determines the impact the identified risks will have on the project and the probability they'll occur, and it puts the risks in priority order according to their effects on the project objectives.
- Be able to define the purpose of Perform Quantitative Risk Analysis. Perform Quantitative Risk Analysis evaluates the impacts of risk prioritized during the Perform

Qualitative Risk Analysis process and quantifies risk exposure for the project by assigning numeric probabilities to each risk and their impacts on project objectives.

- Be able to describe the purpose of the Plan Risk Responses process. Plan Risk Responses is the process where risk response plans are developed using strategies such as escalate, avoid, transfer, mitigate, accept, exploit, share, enhance, develop contingent response strategies, and apply expert judgment. The risk response plan describes the actions to take should the identified risks occur. It should list all the identified risks, a description of the risks, how they'll impact the project objectives, and the people assigned to manage the risk responses.

- Be able to define the risk register and some of its primary elements. The risk register is an output of the Identify Risks process, and updates to the risk register occur as an output of every risk process that follows this one. By the end of the Plan Risk Responses process, the risk register contains these primary elements: identified list of risks, risk owners, risk triggers, risk strategies, contingency plans, and contingency reserves.

- Be able to list the three characteristics of uncertainty. They are product specification, production capability, and process suitability. Choosing an adaptive methodology that allows for small increments of work that produce frequent deliverables, along with frequent reviews of the work, will help manage uncertainty and decrease the chances of rework.

- Be able to state the benefits of frequent reviews practiced in an agile approach as it pertains to risk. Frequent reviews help to increase knowledge among the cross-functional team members, which helps them understand and manage risk.

- Be able to name some of the common issues on projects that could be overcome by using an agile approach. Such issues include unclear team purpose, elusive requirements, poor user participation, unclear estimates and work assignments, poor quality, work and schedule delays, highly complex projects, lack of flexibility, disappointed stakeholders, lack of communication, siloed teams, stop and start workflows.

- Be able to describe the differences in assessing risk when using a predictive vs. an adaptive methodology. The predictive approach requires risk identification, assessment, and preparation of response plans up front, before the work begins. These processes should be repeated throughout the project. Risk identification, assessment, and response planning are performed in each iteration, or workflow stage, of an agile project.

- Be able to describe compliance and why it's important to the project. Compliance involves adhering to laws, regulations, standards, or rules. Failure to adhere to compliance requirements can have devastating consequences to the organization in terms of fines and penalties, lawsuits, damage to reputation, and much more.

- Be certain to work with your stakeholders to identify, prioritize, quantify, assess, and develop action plans for compliance

Planning and procuring resources

- Be able to describe the purpose of the Plan Procurement Management process. The purpose of the Plan Procurement Management process is to identify which project needs should be obtained from outside the organization. Make-or-buy analysis is used as a tool and technique to help determine this.

- Be familiar with the contract types and their usage. Contract types are a tool and technique of the Plan Procurement Management process and include fixed-price and cost reimbursable contracts. Use fixed-price contracts for well- defined projects with a high value to the company, and use cost reimbursable contracts for projects with uncertainty and large investments early in the project life. The three types of fixed price contracts are FFP, FPIF, and FP-EPA. The four types of cost-reimbursable contracts are CPFF, CPIF, CPF (or CPPC), and CPAF. Time and materials contracts are a cross between fixed-price and cost-reimbursable contracts.

- Be familiar with the contract types that help foster a shared-risk-reward relationship. Contract types that work for an agile project help foster a shared-risk-reward relationship between the vendor and the buyer. They include multitiered structure, which entails breaking the contract up into individual documents. Value-driven structure emphasizes having value-driven deliverables rather than meeting a milestone. Fixed-price increments breaks the work down into user stories or releases, and pricing is based on this. Not-to exceed time and materials work on a time and material basis but have an overall contract limit that can't be exceeded. Graduated time and materials rewards the vendor with a higher hourly rate when they exceed contract dates, or reduce the hourly rate when delivery is late. Early cancellation allows the buyer to cancel when further work is no longer needed and typically includes a cancellation fee that is paid to the vendor. Dynamic scope specifies times or points in the project where changes can be made. Team augmentation involves hiring teams of people with the skills needed to work on the project. Favor full-service suppliers involves hiring more than one vendor to work on the project or supply resources to the project.

- Be able to name two of the key elements of procurements on an agile project. Agile projects require close attention to timelines so that purchases are lined up with the agile iterations. Make the vendor resources part of the agile team to help mitigate timing and delivery issues.

- Be able to name the purpose of the Plan Resource Management process. Plan Resource Management involves documenting both human and physical resources needed for the project. Regarding human resources, it documents roles and responsibilities and reporting relationships for the project, and creates the resource plan, which describes how team members are acquired and the criteria for their release. Physical resource needs and time frames are documented here as well.

- Be able to describe an agile team and describe an approach that may help them with training and support. Agile teams are small, cross-functional teams that range from three to nine members. Teams are organized according to strengths, and they are self-organized and self-managed. Agile teams require strong collaboration to help increase productivity, improve creative problem solving, increase knowledge sharing, enable integration of work tasks, and enable flexible work assignments. Establishing agile centers of excellence will help team members with training and support in agile practices.

- Be able to list the benefits of meeting quality requirements. The benefits of meeting quality requirements include increased stakeholder satisfaction, lower costs, higher productivity, and less rework and are discovered during the Plan Quality Management process.

- Be able to define the cost of quality. The COQ is the total cost to produce the product or service of the project according to the quality standards. These costs include all the work necessary to meet the product requirements for quality. The three costs associated with cost of quality are prevention, appraisal, and failure costs (also known as cost of poor quality).

- Be able to name four people associated with COQ and some of the techniques they helped establish. The four are Crosby, Juran, Deming, and Shewhart. Some of the techniques they helped to establish are TQM, Six Sigma, Lean Six Sigma, cost of quality, and continuous improvement. The Kaizen approach concerns continuous improvement and says people should be improved first.

- Be able to describe why quality is built into an agile project. Retrospectives occur at the end of each completed unit of work. The customer examines the work frequently, and inconsistencies and quality issues are identified early on when changes can be made at a lower cost, rather than at the end of the project.

- Be able to name six elemental categories to consider when choosing a life cycle methodology for the project. The six categories are culture, project team, the project itself, needs, complexity, and magnitude.
- Be able to describe complexity. Complexity may involve the skills and ability of the project team, the experience of the project team, unique deliverables or requirements, risk, due dates, costs, business urgency, constraints, and the power and influence of the stakeholders.

Developing the project team

- Be able to identify the distinguishing characteristics of Direct and Manage Project Work. Direct and Manage Project Work is where the work of the project is performed, and the majority of the project budget is spent during this process.
- Name the steps to direct project work on an agile project. The steps are define initial backlog, develop user stories, hold planning meeting, perform daily stand-up meetings, hold review meetings, and conduct retrospective meetings. Retrospectives are the most important practice on any agile project.
- Be able to describe virtual teams. Virtual teams consist of members who work in disparate locations. Virtual workspaces can be used to help engage the teams. The fishbowl window and remote pairing techniques can be used for virtual agile teams. Project managers must continually evaluate the effectiveness of team member engagement on virtual teams.
- Be able to describe generational diversity. Generational diversity involves team members from one of five different generations who may be employed in the workplace today. This includes Silent generation, baby boomers, Gen X, millennials (the largest generation in the workforce today), and Gen Z.
- Be able to describe diversity and inclusion. Diversity involves hiring team members from different

generations, cultures, ethnicities, religious beliefs, sexual orientation, and more. Inclusion involves ensuring that the team is collaborative, supportive, and respectful of one another and that all team members participate on the project and have a voice.

- Be able to name the five stages of group formation. The five stages of group formation are forming, storming, norming, performing, and adjourning.

- Be able to define Maslow's highest level of motivation. Self-actualization occurs when a person performs at their peak and all lower-level needs have been met.

- Know the five types of power. The five types of power are reward, punishment, expert, legitimate, and referent.

- Be able to describe a servant leader. Servant leaders are most common on agile projects. A servant leader leads the team in learning and maturing agile practices by using three steps: purpose, people, and process. A servant leader's main goal is to serve the team and enable the maximum performance possible by the team.

- Know the Shu Ha Ri model. Shu means to obey or protect. Ha means to break free or digress. Ri means to separate or leave. Shu Ha Ri is practiced in somewhat of a progressive fashion.

- Know the difference between "T-Shaped people" and "I-Shaped people." T-Shaped people have a breadth of knowledge and/or experience in several domains. They are also called generalists. I-Shaped people have a breadth and depth of knowledge in a single domain and are called dedicated experts or specialists.

- Be able to describe emotional intelligence. Emotional intelligence is an interpersonal skill that involves knowing and understanding yours and others' emotions. It's a skill all project managers must possess to help promote team performance.

Sharing information

- Be able to describe the purpose of the Implement Risk Responses process. Implement Risk Responses concerns putting the agreed-on risk response plans into action when needed.

- Be able to describe the purpose of the Conduct Procurements process. Conduct Procurements involves obtaining bids and proposals from vendors, selecting a vendor, and awarding a contract.
- Be able to name the contracting life cycle stages. Contracting life cycles include requirement, requisition, solicitation, and award stages.
- Be able to name the type of contract that's best for an agile project. A master service agreement (MSA) is the best type of contract to use for an agile project. Agile projects involve frequent, small deliveries, and an MSA allows you to add work to the contract via an appendix without having to rewrite the contract.
- Be able to describe the purpose of the Manage Quality process. The Manage Quality process is concerned with making certain the project will meet and satisfy the quality standards of the project.
- Be able to describe managing quality on an agile project. Quality criteria are part of the acceptance criteria and define a completed work unit.
- Quality on agile teams is higher due to shortened time frames, small deliverables, and automated testing, and outside dependencies are eliminated.
- Be able to describe automated code quality analysis. A method of testing code using scripts that review the code line by line to identify bugs or vulnerabilities in the programming code.
- Be able to name the steps involved in managing project artifacts. Determine the requirements for managing project artifacts, apply version controls, make artifacts accessible to all stakeholders, and continually monitor and assess the processes involved in managing artifacts.
- Be able to differentiate between senders and receivers of information. Senders are responsible for clear, concise, complete messages, whereas receivers are responsible for understanding the message correctly.
- Be able to describe the sender-receiver model and the interactive communication model. The

sender-receiver model involves a sender who encodes and transmits a message and a receiver who decodes and interprets the message. The interactive communication model includes the sender-receiver model as well as an acknowledgment that the message was received and feedback regarding the contents of the message.

- Be able to describe the purpose of the Manage Communication process. Manage Communication involves making sure project information is available to stakeholders at the right time and in the appropriate format.
- Be able to identify the five stages of conflict defined by Louis Pondy. The five stages are latent, perceived, felt, manifest, and aftermath. Be able to identify the five styles of conflict resolution. The five styles of conflict resolution are force/direct, smooth/accommodate, compromise/reconcile, collaborate/problem solve, and withdraw/avoid.
- Be able to describe the purpose of the Manage Project Knowledge process. Manage Project Knowledge involves sharing organizational as well as project knowledge and creating new knowledge that can be shared in the future in order to increase the chance for success for the project.

- Be able to name the most important benefit of communicating with and providing project artifacts to stakeholders. This helps ensure stakeholders are engaged and informed. This is critical for project success.
- Be able to describe the purpose of the Manage Stakeholder Engagement process. Manage Stakeholder Engagement involves satisfying the needs of the stakeholders and successfully meeting the goals of the project by managing communications with stakeholders, resolving issues, engaging them on the project, managing their expectations, improving project performance by implementing requested changes, and managing concerns in anticipation of potential problems.
- Be able to name the purpose of an agile scaling framework. This allows for scaling agile from individual teams to the enterprise.

- Be able to name some popular agile scaling frameworks. These include Scrum of Scrums, Large-Scale Scrum, Enterprise Scrum, Scaled Agile Framework, and Disciplined Agile.

Measuring and controlling project performance

- Describe the purpose of the Monitor and Control Project Work process. This process is responsible for reviewing, tracking, and controlling project progress.
- Name the processes that integrate with the Control Procurements process. These processes are Direct and Manage Project Work, Monitor Communications, Control Quality, Perform Integrated Change Control, and Monitor Risks.
- Describe the purpose of the Monitor Communications process. Monitor Communications concerns monitoring and controlling communications throughout the life of the project.
- Name the purpose of the Perform Integrated Change Control process. Perform Integrated Change Control is performed throughout the life of the project and involves reviewing all the project change requests, establishing a configuration management and change control process, and approving or denying changes.
- Be able to define the purpose of a configuration management system. Configuration management systems are documented procedures that describe the process for submitting change requests, the processes for tracking changes and their disposition, and the processes for defining the approval levels for approving and denying changes. The configuration management system also includes a process for authorizing the changes. Change control systems are generally a subset of the configuration management system. Configuration management also describes the characteristics of the product of the project and ensures the accuracy and completeness of the description.
- Be able to describe a CCB. The change control board (CCB) has the authority to approve or deny change requests. Their authority is

defined and outlined by the organization. A CCB is made up of stakeholders.

- Be able to describe the purpose of the Monitor Stakeholder Engagement process. The purpose is to monitor stakeholder relationships and ensure their continued engagement in the project.
- Be able to name the purpose of the Control Resources process. The purpose of Control Resources is to make certain the right physical resources are available at the time they are needed and at the location they are needed. This process also ensures that the resources are released when their job is completed and that corrective actions are taken when resources are not utilized as planned.
- Be able to name the purpose of the Control Quality process. The purpose of the Control Quality process is to monitor work results to see whether they comply with the standards set out in the quality management plan.
- Describe the purpose of Monitor Risks. Monitor Risks involves identifying and responding to new risks

as they occur. Risk monitoring and reassessment should occur throughout the life of the project.

- Describe the purpose of monitoring project integrations. You should review the tailoring processes and determine whether they are delivering the efficiencies you expected. You should document your findings in the lessons learned document for future reference. Some elements to examine include project and development life cycles, change management, lessons learned, and reporting on expected benefits.

Controlling work results and closing out the project

- Name the purpose of the Control Costs process. The Control Costs process is concerned with monitoring project costs to prevent unauthorized or incorrect costs from being included in the cost baseline.
- Be able to describe earned value management techniques. Earned value management (EVM) monitors the planned value (PV), earned value (EV), and

actual costs (AC) expended to produce the work of the project. Cost variance (CV), schedule variance (SV), cost performance index (CPI), and schedule performance index (SPI) are the formulas used with the EVM technique.

- Name the purpose of the Validate Scope process. The purpose of Validate Scope is to determine whether the work is complete and whether it satisfies the project objectives. Validate Scope should be performed for both predictive and agile projects when a project is canceled.

- Be able to describe product verification. Product verification confirms that all the work of the project was completed accurately and to the satisfaction of the stakeholder. This is performed at the end of an iteration or flow-based work period on agile projects.

- Be able to name the primary activity of the Close Project or Phase process. The key activity of this process is concerned with completing all the activities associated with closing out the project management processes in order to officially close out the project or phase. It also ensures that all project work is complete.

- Be able to describe when the Close Project or Phase process is performed. Close Project or Phase is performed at the close of each project phase and at the close of the project.

- Be able to define the purpose of lessons learned. The purpose of lessons learned is to describe the project successes and failures and to use the information learned on future projects.

- Be able to name several measures used on agile projects. Measure include the following: definition of done (DoD) defines exit criteria for the iteration; definition of ready (DoR) is entry criteria for the iteration; capacity measures (such as burndown and burnup charts) measure velocity; empirical measures are usually expressed as deliverables, functionality, or features; cycle time is a flow-based measure that calculates the time it takes for a task to complete work; lead time is a flow based measure that calculates the time it takes for a task to complete work from request to completion; and response time is a flow-based measure that calculates the time a task waits to start work.

- Be able to describe the steps to close out an agile project. Examine criteria to close; obtain final acceptance of deliverables; obtain legal, financial, procurement, and administrative closure; update and archive all project documents; hold a final retrospective and a final lessons learned meeting; prepare and distribute final project report; validate readiness for transition; ensure knowledge transfer; confirm approach for knowledge transfer; and release team members.
- Be able to name the publication that describes the ethical standards to which PMP® credential holders are required to adhere. The ethical standards PMP® credential holders are required to adhere to are described in the PMI® Code of Ethics and Professional Conduct.
- Describe the areas in which PMP® credential holders must apply professional knowledge. PMP® credential holders must apply professional

knowledge in the areas of project management practices, industry practices, and technical areas.
- Know the key activity that ensures customer satisfaction. The key activity that ensures customer satisfaction is documenting project requirements and meeting them.

Performance Domain I: Initiating

- Perform project assessment based on available information, lessons learned from previous projects, and meetings with relevant stakeholders in order to support evaluation of the feasibility of new products or services within the given assumptions and/or constraints.
- Identify key deliverables based on the business requirements in order to manage customer expectations and direct the achievement of project goals.
- Perform stakeholder analysis using appropriate tools and techniques in order to align expectations and gain support for the project.
- Identify high-level risks, assumptions, and

constraints based on the current environment, organizational factors, historical data, and expert judgment, in order to propose an implementation strategy.

- Participate in the development of the project charter by compiling and analyzing gathered information in order to ensure project stakeholders are in agreement on its elements.
- Obtain project charter approval from the sponsor, in order to formalize the authority assigned to the project manager and gain commitment and acceptance for the project.
- Conduct benefit analysis with relevant stakeholders to validate project alignment with organizational strategy and expected business value.
- Inform stakeholders of the approved project charter to ensure common understanding of the key deliverables, milestones, and their roles and responsibilities.

Performance Domain II: Planning

- Review and assess detailed project requirements, constraints, and assumptions with stakeholders based on the project charter, lessons learned, and by using requirement gathering techniques in order to establish detailed project deliverables.
- Develop a scope management plan, based on the approved project scope and using scope management techniques, in order to define, maintain, and manage the scope of the project.
- Develop the cost management plan based on the project scope, schedule, resources, approved project charter and other information, using estimating techniques, in order to manage project costs.
- Develop the project schedule based on the approved project deliverables and milestones, scope, and resource management plans in order to manage timely completion of the project.
- Develop the human resource management plan by defining the roles and responsibilities of the project team members in order to create a project

organizational structure and provide guidance regarding how resources will be assigned and managed.

- Develop the communications management plan based on the project organizational structure and stakeholder requirements, in order to define and manage the flow of project information.
- Develop the procurement management plan based on the project scope, budget, and schedule, in order to ensure that the required project resources will be available.
- Develop the quality management plan and define the quality standards for the project and its products, based on the project scope, risks, and requirements, in order to prevent the occurrence of defects and control the cost of quality.
- Develop the change management plan by defining how changes will be addressed and controlled in order to track and manage change.
- Plan for risk management by developing a risk management plan; identifying, analyzing, and prioritizing project risks;

creating the risk register; and defining risk response strategies in order to manage uncertainty and opportunity throughout the project life cycle.

- Present the project management plan to the relevant stakeholders according to applicable policies and procedures in order to obtain approval to proceed with project execution.
- Conduct kickoff meeting, communicating the start of the project, key milestones, and other relevant information in order to inform and engage stakeholders and gain commitment.
- Develop the stakeholder management plan by analyzing needs, interests, and potential impact in order to effectively manage stakeholders' expectations and engage them in project decisions.

Performance Domain III: Executing

- Acquire and manage project resources by following the human resource and procurement management plans in order to meet project requirements.
- Manage task execution based on the project

management plan by leading and developing the project team in order to achieve project deliverables.

- Implement the quality management plan using the appropriate tools and techniques in order to ensure that work is performed in accordance with required quality standards.
- Implement approved changes and corrective actions by following the change management plan in order to meet project requirements.
- Implement approved actions by following the risk management plan in order to minimize the impact of the risks and take advantage of opportunities on the project.
- Manage the flow of information by following the communications plan in order to keep stakeholders engaged and informed.
- Maintain stakeholder relationships by following the stakeholder management plan in order to receive continued support and manage expectations.

Performance Domain IV: Monitoring and Controlling

- Measure project performance using appropriate tools and techniques in order to identify and quantify any variances and corrective actions.
- Manage changes to the project by following the change management plan in order to ensure that project goals remain aligned with business needs.
- Verify that project deliverables conform to the quality standards established in the quality management plan by using appropriate tools and techniques to meet project requirements and business needs.
- Monitor and assess risk by determining whether exposure has changed and evaluating the effectiveness of response strategies in order to manage the impact of risks and opportunities to the project.
- Review the issue log, update if necessary, and determine corrective actions by using appropriate tools and techniques in order to minimize the impact on the project.

- Capture, analyze, and manage lessons learned using lessons learned management techniques in order to enable continuous improvement.
- Monitor procurement activities according to the procurement plan in order to verify compliance with project objectives.

Performance Domain V: Closing
- Obtain final acceptance of the project deliverables from relevant stakeholders in order to confirm that project scope and deliverables were achieved.
- Transfer the ownership of deliverables to the assigned stakeholders in accordance with the project plan in order to facilitate project closure.
- Obtain financial, legal, and administrative closure using generally accepted practices and policies in order to communicate formal project closure and ensure transfer of liability.
- Prepare and share the final project report according to the communications management plan in order to document and convey project performance and assist in project evaluation.

- Collate lessons learned that were documented throughout the project and conduct a comprehensive project review in order to update the organization's knowledge base.
- Archive project documents and materials using generally accepted practices in order to comply with statutory requirements and for potential use in future projects and audits.
- Obtain feedback from relevant stakeholders using appropriate tools and techniques and based on the stakeholder management plan in order to evaluate their satisfaction.

Exam Questions

1. You work for Writer's Block, a service that reviews and critiques manuscripts for aspiring writers. You were assigned to be the project manager for a new computer system that logs, tracks, and electronically scans and files all submitted manuscripts along with the editor's notes. You hired a vendor to perform this project, and they used an agile methodology to manage the project. You are documenting how well the tailoring processes and project integration worked for this project. Which of the following information will you document regarding project integration?

   A. You documented the project life cycle and development life cycle you used to manage the project.

   B. You documented the management approaches used on the project.

   C. You documented the expected benefits to ensure the intended benefits were brought about on the project.

   D. You documented how project knowledge was managed.

   E. B, C, D

   F. A, B, C, D

2. The project sponsor has approached you with a dilemma. At the annual stockholders' meeting, the CEO announced that the project you're managing will be completed by the end of this year. The problem is that this is six months prior to the scheduled completion date. It's too late to go back and correct her mistake, and now stockholders expect implementation by the announced date. You must speed up the delivery date of this project. Your primary constraint before this occurred was the budget. Choose the best action from the options listed to speed up the project.

   A. Hire more resources to get the work completed faster.

   B. Ask for more money so that you can contract out one of the phases you had planned to do with in-house resources.

   C. Utilize negotiation and influencing skills to convince the project sponsor to speak with the CEO and make a correction to her announcement.

   D. Examine the project management plan to see

whether there are any phases that can be fast tracked, and then revise the project management plan to reflect the compression of the schedule.

3. These types of dependencies can create arbitrary total float values and limit your scheduling options.
A. Discretionary
B. External
C. Mandatory
D. Hard logic

4. Project managers spend what percentage of their time communicating?
A. 90
B. 85
C. 75
D. 50

5. Match the following agile measurements with their definitions.
Agile measurements and definitions
Agile measurements
Definitions

A. Definition of done	1. The time a task waits before work starts
B. Empirical measure	2. A type of in-the-moment measure
C. Lead time	3. Describes the specifics of the tasks planned for the iteration before the team begins work
D. Definition of ready	4. The time it takes for a task to go from request to completion
E. Response time	5. The time it takes to complete work on a task from the time work starts
F. Cycle time	6. A checklist of elements needed to ensure the deliverable is ready for the customer to use

G. Capacity measures	7. Typically expressed as deliverables, functionality, or features

6. Your project has a high degree of certainty, firm requirements, a stable team, and low risk. Which of the following life cycle methodologies does this describe?
A. Flow-based agile
B. XP
C. Six Sigma DMAIC
D. Predictive

7. Which of the following statements regarding configuration management is not true?
A. Configuration management involves managing changes to the project baselines.
B. Change control systems are a subset of the configuration management system.
C. Configuration management focuses on the specifications of the deliverables of the project.
D. Configuration management validates and improves the project by evaluating the impact of each change.

8. Name the difference between the agile iterative approach and the agile incremental approach as discussed in the Agile Practice Guide (PMI®, 2017).
A. Incremental uses prototypes and iterative helps in performing the work faster and in speeding up the project.
B. Incremental focuses on learning optimization and iterative focuses on speed of delivery.
C. Iterative plans the work at the beginning of the project before starting work, and incremental plans the work at the beginning of each iteration.
D. Iterative uses prototypes and incremental helps in performing the work faster and speeding up the project.

9. Your project has a high degree of uncertainty, high risk, evolving requirements, and cross-functional teams. Which of the following life cycle methodologies does this describe?
A. Agile
B. Hybrid
C. Predictive

D. Waterfall

10. During your project meeting, a problem was discussed, and a resolution to the problem was reached. During the meeting, the participants started wondering why they thought the problem was such a big issue. Sometime after the meeting, you received an email from one of the meeting participants saying they've changed their mind about the solution reached in the meeting and need to resurface the problem. The solution reached during the initial project meeting is a result of which of the following conflict resolution techniques?
A. Collaborate
B. Forcing
C. Smoothing
D. Storming

11. According to the PMBOK® Guide, which of the following names all the components of an interactive communication model?
A. Encode, transmit, decode
B. Encode, transmit, decode, acknowledge, feedback/response
C. Encode, transmit, decode, feedback/response
D. Encode, transmit, acknowledge, decode

12. What are benefit measurement methods?
A. Project selection criteria
B. Project selection methods
C. Project selection committees
D. Project resource and budget selection methods

13. During your project meeting, a problem was discussed, and the project sponsor described the resolution they wanted the project team to implement. The project manager tried to interject with another idea that might solve the issues but the sponsor didn't want to discuss the idea. Which of the following conflict resolution techniques does this question describe?
A. Collaborate
B. Forcing
C. Smoothing
D. Storming

14. Which of the following factors are changes that occur to the external business environment that may impact the

organization and your project?
A. Mergers and acquisitions
B. Geopolitical and marketplace
C. Regulatory and technology
D. Social and economic
E. A, C, D F. A, B, C, D

15. You've been assigned as a project manager on a research and development project for a new dental procedure. You're working in the Project Scope Management Knowledge Area. What is the purpose of the scope management plan?
A. The scope management plan describes and documents a scope baseline to help make future project decisions.
B. The scope management plan decomposes project deliverables into smaller units of work.
C. The scope management plan describes how project scope will be developed and how scope changes will be managed.
D. The scope management plan describes how cost and time estimates will be developed for project scope changes.

16. Which of the following statements regarding Ishikawa diagrams are true?
A. Ishikawa diagrams are also called cause-and-effect diagrams.
B. Ishikawa diagrams are also called fishbone diagrams.
C. Ishikawa diagrams help identify the root cause of the problem.
D. Ishikawa diagrams are also known as why-why diagrams.
E. A, B, C, D F. A, B, D

17. What is one of the most important skills a project manager can have?
A. Negotiation skills
B. Influencing skills
C. Communication skills
D. Business skills

18. Which of the following terms are other names for inspections?
A. Reviews
B. Assessment
C. Walk-through
D. Audits
E. A, C, D F. A, B, C, D

19. You are the project manager for Xylophone Phonics. It produces children's software programs that teach basic reading and

math skills. You're performing cost estimates for your project and don't have a lot of details yet. Which of the following techniques should you use?

A. Analogous estimating techniques, because this is a form of expert judgment that uses historical information from similar projects

B. Bottom-up estimating techniques, because this is a form of expert judgment that uses historical information from similar projects

C. Monte Carlo analysis, because this is a modeling technique that uses simulation to determine estimates

D. Parametric modeling, because this is a form of simulation used to determine estimates

20. Project managers have the highest level of authority and the most power in which type of organizational structure?

A. Project-oriented
B. Simple
C. Functional
D. Hybrid

21. This process is concerned with determining the engagement levels of the stakeholders.

A. Plan Communications Management
B. Control Communications
C. Plan Stakeholder Engagement
D. Manage Stakeholder Engagement

22. All of the following statements are true regarding risk events except which one?

A. Project risks are uncertain events.

B. If risks occur, they can have a positive or negative effect on project objectives.

C. Unknown risks can be threats to the project objectives, and nothing can be done to plan for them.

D. Risks that have more perceived rewards to the organization than consequences should be accepted.

23. Which of the following describes the key focus or purpose of the Manage Project Knowledge process?

A. Gathering, creating, storing, distributing, retrieving, and disposing of project information

B. Managing communications, resolving issues, engaging others on the project, managing expectations, improving project performance by implementing requested changes, and managing concerns in anticipation of potential problems

C. Sharing organizational and project knowledge and creating new knowledge that can be shared in the future

D. Performing systematic activities to determine which processes should be used to achieve the project requirements, and to ensure that activities and processes are performed efficiently and effectively

24. You are the project manager for Xylophone Phonics. This company produces children's software programs that teach basic reading and math skills. You are ready to assign project roles, responsibilities, and reporting relationships.

    On which project Planning process are you working?

    A. Estimate Activity Resources

    B. Plan Resource Management

    C. Acquire Project Team

    D. Plan Organizational Resources

25. Match the following types of tests that are used on agile-based software projects to their description. Testing at all levels Name of test Description

    A. Integration test 1. Testing the software from the start to the end to ensure the application is working correctly.

    B. End-to end test 2. A high-level test designed to identify simple failures that could jeopardize the software program.

    C. Regression test 3. This test is performed after changes are made to the code or when maintenance activities are performed on the hardware the code resides on to ensure the software works the same way it did before the change.

    D. Unit test 4. This test combines software modules and tests them as a group.

    E. Smoke test 5. This test is performed on individual modules or individual components of source code.

26. These types of meetings are associated with the agile project management methodologies. They occur at the beginning of an iteration. Team members choose items from the backlog list to work on during the iteration. What is this meeting called?

A. Review planning meeting

B. Planning meeting

C. Retrospective planning meeting

D. Daily stand-up planning meeting

27. These diagrams rank-order factors for corrective action by frequency of occurrence. They are also a type of histogram.

A. Control charts

B. Process flowcharts

C. Scatter diagrams

D. Pareto diagrams

28. You are a project manager who has recently held a project team kickoff meeting where all the team members were formally introduced to each other. Some of the team members know each other from other projects and have been working with you for the past three weeks. Which of the following statements is not true?

A. Team building improves the knowledge and skills of team members.

B. Team building builds feelings of trust and agreement among team members, which can improve morale.

C. Team building can create a dynamic environment and cohesive culture to improve productivity of both the team and the project.

D. Team building occurs throughout the life of the project and can establish clear expectations and behaviors for project team members, leading to increased productivity.

29. You are a project manager for the Swirling Seas Cruises food division. You're considering two different projects regarding food services on the cruise lines. The initial cost of Project Fish'n for Chips will be $800,000, with expected cash inflows of $300,000 per quarter. Project Picnic's payback period is six months. Which project should you recommend?

A. Project Fish'n for Chips, because its payback period is two months shorter than Project Picnic's

B. Project Fish'n for Chips, because the costs on Project Picnic are unknown

C. Project Picnic, because Project Fish'n for Chips's payback period is four months longer than Project Picnic's

D. Project Picnic, because Project Fish'n for Chips's payback period is two months longer than Project Picnic's

30. Which of the following compression techniques increases risk?
    A. Crashing
    B. Resource leveling
    C. Fast-tracking
    D. Lead and lag

31. You are the project manager for a construction company that is building a new city and county office building in your city. You recently looked over the construction site to determine whether the work to date conformed to the requirements and quality standards. Which tool and technique of the Control Quality process were you using?
    A. Defect repair review
    B. Inspection
    C. Sampling
    D. Quality audit

32. You have been assigned to a project that will allow job seekers to fill out applications and submit them via the company website. You report to the VP of human resources. You are also responsible for screening applications for the information technology division and setting up interviews. The project coordinator has asked for the latest version of your changes to the online application page for his review. Which organizational structure do you work in?
    A. Functional organization
    B. Weak matrix organization
    C. Virtual organization
    D. Balanced matrix organization

33. The primary function of the Closing processes is to perform all of the following except which one?
    A. Formalize lessons learned and distribute this information to project participants.
    B. Complete all activities associated with closing out the project.
    C. Validate that the deliverables are complete and accurate.
    D. Ensure all project work is complete and accurate.

34. You are the project manager for Lucky Stars Candies. You've identified the requirements for the project and documented them where?
    A. In the requirements documentation, which will be used as an input to the Create WBS process
    B. In the project scope statement, which is used as an input to the Create WBS process

C. In the product requirements document, which is an output of the Define Scope process

D. In the project specifications document, which is an output of the Define Scope process

35. What is the purpose of the project charter?

A. To recognize and acknowledge the project sponsor

B. To recognize and acknowledge the existence of the project and commit organizational resources to the project

C. To acknowledge the existence of the project team, project manager, and project sponsor

D. To describe the selection methods used to choose this project over its competitors

36. Which of the following are tools and techniques of the Identify Stakeholders process you can use to categorize stakeholders? (Choose two.)

A. Salience model

B. Power/interest grid

C. Stakeholder register

D. Stakeholder engagement assessment

37. You are a project manager working on a software development project. You've developed the risk management plan, identified risks, and determined risk responses for the risks. A risk event occurs, and you implement the response. Then, another risk event occurs as a result of the response you implemented. What type of risk is this?

A. Trigger risk

B. Residual risk

C. Secondary risk

D. Mitigated risk

38. All of the following are a type of project ending except for which one?

A. Extinction

B. Starvation

C. Desertion

D. Addition

39. You are working on a project that will upgrade the phone system in your customer service center. You have considered using analogous estimating, parametric estimating, bottom-up estimating, and three-point estimating to determine activity costs. Which process does this describe?

A. Estimating Activity Resources

B. Estimate Costs

C. Determine Budget

D. Estimating Activity Costs

40. Failure costs are also known as which of the following?

A. Internal costs

B. Cost of poor quality

C. Cost of keeping defects out of the hands of customers

D. Prevention costs

41. Feeding buffers and the project buffer are part of which of the following Develop Schedule tool and technique?

A. Critical path method

B. Schedule network analysis

C. Applying leads and lags

D. Critical chain method

42. You are the project manager for a construction company that is building a new city and county office building in your city. Your CCB recently approved a scope change. You know that scope change might come about as a result of all of the following except which one?

A. Schedule revisions

B. Product scope change

C. Changes to the agreed-on WBS

D. Changes to the project requirements

43. You are working on a project that will upgrade the phone system in your customer service center. You have used bottom-up estimating techniques to assign costs to the project activities and have determined the cost baseline. Which of the following statements is true?

A. You have completed the Estimate Cost process and now need to complete the Determine Budget process to develop the project's cost baseline.

B. You have completed the Estimate Cost process and established a cost baseline to measure future projects against.

C. You have completed the Determine Budget process and now need to complete the Schedule Development process to establish a project baseline to measure future project performance against.

D. You have completed the Determine Budget process, and the cost baseline will be used to measure future project performance.

44. Each of the following options describes an element of the Develop Project Management Plan process except for which one?

A. Project charter

B. Outputs from other planning processes

C. Configuration management system

D. Organizational process assets

45. This type of leader leads the team in learning and maturing agile practices. They promote emotional intelligence and selfawareness, they are good listeners, put the needs of others first, help team members improve their skills, they coach and mentor, encourage safety, encourage respectful behaviors, build trust among the team, and promote the skills and intelligence of others. Which of the following leadership styles does this question describe and what are the three steps, in order, they use to help the team learn and mature agile processes? (Choose two.)

A. This question describes a servant leader.

B. This type of leader takes these steps in this order: people, purpose, and process.

C. This question describes a democratic leader.

D. This type of leader takes these three steps in this order: purpose, people, process.

46. Monte Carlo analysis can help predict the impact of risks on project deliverables. It is an element of one of the tools and techniques of one of the following processes. The other tools and techniques of this process include sensitivity analysis, decision tree analysis, and influence diagrams.

A. Plan Risk Responses

B. Perform Quantitative Risk Analysis

C. Identify Risks

D. Perform Qualitative Risk Analysis

47. You know that PV = 470, AC = 430, EV = 460, EAC = 500, and BAC = 525. What is VAC?

A. 65

B. 20

C. 25

D. 30

48. Which of the following contracts should you use for agile projects that will be priced based on user stories?

A. Multitiered structure

B. Dynamic scope

C. Graduated time and materials

D. Fixed-price increments

49. Every status meeting should have time allotted for reviewing risks. Which of the following options are true?

A. Risk identification and monitoring should occur throughout the life of the project.
B. Risk audits are performed during the Monitoring and Controlling phase of the project.
C. Risks should be monitored for their status and to determine whether the impacts to the objectives have changed.
D. Technical performance measurement variances may indicate that a risk is looming and should be reviewed at status meetings.
E. A, C, D F. A, B, C, D

50. Name the two types of agile approaches discussed in the Agile Practice Guide (PMI®, 2017).
A. Iteration-based and flow-based
B. Hybrid and incremental-based
C. Incremental-based and agile
D. Predictive-based and release planning–based

51. Name the ethical code you'll be required to adhere to as a PMP® credential holder.
A. Project Management Policy and Ethics Code
B. PMI® Standards and Ethics Code of Conduct
C. Project Management Code of Professional Ethics
D. PMI® Code of Ethics and Professional Conduct

52. According to the PMBOK® Guide, the project manager is identified and assigned during which process?
A. During the Develop Project Charter process
B. At the conclusion of the Develop Project Charter process
C. Prior to beginning the Planning processes
D. Prior to beginning the Define Scope process

53. The project manager is responsible for all of the following regarding business value except which one?
A. Delivering the project so business value can be realized
B. Work with the team to subdivide tasks into the minimum viable product whenever possible
C. Measuring business value
D. Delivering business value at the end of the project

54. Which of the following statements are true regarding risks?
A. Risks might be threats to the objectives of the project.
B. Risks are certain events that may be threats or

opportunities to the objectives of the project.

C. Risks might be opportunities to the objectives of the project.

D. Risks have causes and consequences.

E. A, C, D

55. Shu Ha Ri is a technique used to develop an agile team. Which of the following are true about this model?

A. Shu stage means to obey or protect.

B. Ha stage means to separate or leave.

C. Ri stage means to break free or digress.

D. Shu Ha Ri comes from Aikido, a Japanese martial art form.

E. Shu Ha Ri is practiced in a progressive fashion.

F. A, D, E G. A, B, D, E

56. Match the following scaling agile frameworks with their description. Scaling agile frameworks Framework Description

A. LeSS 1. Two or more Scrum teams work on the project together. Each Scrum team focuses on a portion of the work.

B. SAFe 2. This consists of up to eight Scrum teams with up to eight members each who all work on the project together.

C. Enterprise Scrum 3. This extends Scrum practices to all aspects of the organization.

D. Scrum of Scrums 4. This combines several agile best practices and includes information from functional areas of the business. Framework Description E. DA 5. This is an interactive knowledge base consisting of technical guidance, knowledge, and information on agile.

57. Which performance measurement tells you what the projected total cost of the project will be at completion?

A. ETC

B. EV

C. AC

D. EAC

58. Which of the following statements is true regarding the Project Management Knowledge Areas?

A. They include Initiation, Planning, Executing, Monitoring and Controlling, and Closing.

B. They consist of 10 areas that bring together processes that have things in common.

C. They consist of five processes that bring together phases of projects that have things in common.

D. They include Planning, Executing, and Monitoring and Controlling processes because these three processes are commonly interlinked.

59. What are the Define Scope process tools and techniques?

A. Cost–benefit analysis, scope baseline, expert judgment, and facilitated workshops

B. Product analysis, alternatives generation, and expert judgment

C. Product analysis, alternatives analysis, expert judgment, multicriteria decision analysis, and facilitation

D. Alternatives generation, stakeholder analysis, and expert judgment

60. You are the project manager for Heartthrobs by the Numbers Dating Services. You're working on an updated website that will display pictures as well as short bios of prospective heartbreakers. You have your activity list and resource requirements in hand. You are using an adaptive methodology to manage the project. Which of the following is true?

A. A Kanban Board is capacity based.

B. A Scrum Board is time or velocity based.

C. A burndown chart will show the remaining work of the sprint.

D. All of the above.

61. Which performance measurement tells you the cost of the work that has been authorized and budgeted for a WBS component?

A. PV

B. EV

C. AC

D. BCWP

62. Your team is developing the risk management plan. Which tool and technique of this process is used to develop risk cost elements and schedule activities that will be included in the project budget and schedule?

A. Meetings

B. Data analysis

C. Information-gathering techniques

D. Risk data quality assessment

63. You are the project manager for Xylophone Phonics. It produces children's software programs that teach basic reading and math skills. You are performing the Plan Quality Management process and are identifying

operational definitions. Which of the following does this describe?

A. The quality metrics

B. The quality management plan

C. The project documents update

D. The cost of quality

64. You need to convey some very complex, detailed information to the project stakeholders. What is the best method for communicating this kind of information?

A. Verbal

B. Vertical

C. Horizontal

D. Written

65. You have just prepared an RFP for release. Your project involves a substantial amount of contract work detailed in the RFP. Your favorite vendor drops by and offers to give you and your spouse the use of their company condo for your upcoming vacation. It's located in a beautiful resort community that happens to be one of your favorite places to go for a getaway. What is the most appropriate response?

A. Thank the vendor, but decline the offer because you know this could be considered a conflict of interest.

B. Thank the vendor, and accept. This vendor is always offering you incentives like this, so this offer does not likely have anything to do with the recent RFP release.

C. Thank the vendor, accept the offer, and immediately tell your project sponsor so they're aware of what you're doing.

D. Thank the vendor, but decline the offer because you've already made another arrangement for this vacation. Ask them whether you can take a rain check and arrange another time to use the condo.

66. Directing project work on an agile project consists of several steps. Match the following steps with their descriptions.

67. **Directing agile teamwork**

Steps	Description
A. First step	1. Review meetings are held to examine the work of the iteration and provide and receive feedback
B. Second step	2. Daily stand-ups are conducted to examine what was worked on yesterday, what will be worked on today, and what obstacles are standing in the way.
C. Third step	3. The product backlog is defined.
D. Fourth step	4. Retrospectives are held at the end of the iteration to determine what went well, what improvements can be made to the process, and what didn't go well.
E. Fifth step	5. Planning meetings are held at the beginning of the iteration to pull user stories into the iteration backlog.

68. You are a project manager for Waterways Houseboats, Inc. You've been asked to perform a cost–benefit analysis for two proposed projects. Project A costs $2.4 million, with potential benefits of $12 million and future operating costs of $3 million. Project B costs $2.8 million, with potential benefits of $14 million and future operating costs of $2 million. Which project should you recommend?

A. Project A, because the cost to implement it is cheaper than with Project B

B. Project A, because the potential benefits plus the future operating costs are less in value than the same calculation for Project B

C. Project B, because the potential benefits minus the implementation and future operating costs are greater in value than the same calculation for Project A

D. Project B, because the potential benefits minus the costs to implement are greater in value than the same calculation for Project A

69. Louis R. Pondy, a professor of business administration and author on organizational management and other topics, developed the stages of conflict. Which of the following are stages of conflict according to Pondy? (Choose three.)

A. Collaborate
B. Latent
C. Avoid
D. Felt
E. Perceived

70. You are performing alternatives analysis as part of the Define Scope process. Which of the following options is not true?

A. Alternatives analysis is a component of the data analysis tool and technique.

B. Alternatives analysis is used in the Plan Scope Management process and the Define Scope process.

C. Alternatives analysis involves unanimity, plurality, majority, and autocratic voting methods.

D. Brainstorming and lateral thinking are types of alternative analysis.

71. The project manager has the greatest influence over quality during which process?

A. Plan Quality Management
B. Manage Quality
C. Control Quality
D. Monitor Quality

72. What type of organization experiences the least amount of stress during project closeout?

A. Project-oriented
B. Functional
C. Weak matrix
D. Strong matrix

73. You are working on the product description for your company's new line of ski boots. Your customers have been asking for changes in style. New advances in the manufacturing process allows you to make these changes quickly and get the new line on the shelves before the next ski season. Your organization hopes to increase revenues and market share by offering this new line of boots.

Which of the following are true? (Choose two.)

A. One KPI used to measure business value might be improving the organization's business relationship with the manufacturer.

B. The business value for this project is increasing revenues and market share.

C. This project came about due to an organizational need to add a new style of boots and get them to market quickly.

D. This project came about as a result of a customer request and technological advance.

74. The business need or demand that brought about the project, high-level scope description, analysis of the problem or opportunity the project presents, recommendation, and an evaluation statement together describe elements of which of the following?

A. Organizational process assets

B. The feasibility study

C. The business case

D. The project charter

75. Which of the following statements is true regarding constraints and assumptions?

A. Constraints restrict the actions of the project team, and assumptions are considered true for planning purposes.

B. Constraints are considered true for planning purposes, and assumptions limit the options of the project team.

C. Constraints consider vendor availability and resource availability to be true for planning purposes. Assumptions limit the project team to work within predefined budgets or timelines.

D. Constraints and assumptions are inputs to the Initiation process. They should be documented because they will be used throughout the project planning process.

76. People are motivated by the need for achievement, power, or affiliation according to which theory?

A. Expectancy Theory

B. Achievement Theory

C. Contingency Theory

D. Theory X

77. You are a project manager working in a foreign country. You observe that some of your project team members are having a difficult time adjusting to the new culture. You

provided them with training on cultural differences and the customs of this country before they arrived, but they still seem uncomfortable and disoriented. Which of the following statements is true?

A. This is the result of working with teams of people from two different countries.

B. This condition is known as culture shock.

C. This is the result of jet lag and travel fatigue.

D. This condition is known as global culturalism.

78. As a result of a face-to-face meeting you recently had to discuss the items in your issue log, you have resolved issues, managed expectations, and come away with an action plan that will improve project performance and will also require an update to the communications management plan. Which process does this describe?

A. Manage Stakeholder Engagement

B. Control Communications

C. Manage Project Communications

D. Manage Team

79. Which of the following are a type of agile project management methodology primarily used for information technology projects? (Choose two.) A. Scrum B. Six Sigma C. XP D. Kaizen

80. What is the definition of free float?

A. The amount of time you can delay the earliest start of a task without delaying the ending of the project

B. The amount of time you can delay the start of a task without delaying the earliest start of a successor task

C. The amount of time you can delay the latest start of a task without delaying the ending of the project

D. The amount of time you can delay the start of a task without delaying the earliest finish of a successor task

81. Generational diversity is an important component of diversity and inclusion when building your team. Which of the following are true statements about the five generations in the workplace today? (Choose two.)

A. Baby Boomers experienced rationing of food, gas, and other everyday items while growing up. They are often frugal and strong savers.

B. Millennials are also known as the "latchkey" generation.

C. Gen X are also known as the "MTV" generation.

D. Gen Z grew up with technology as a way of life and are heavily influenced by social media.

82. Your project involves the research and development of a new food additive. You're ready to release the product to your customer when you discover that a minor reaction might occur in people with certain conditions. The reactions to date have been very minor, and no known long-lasting side effects have been noted. As project manager, what should you do?

A. Do nothing because the reactions are so minor that very few people will be affected.

B. Inform the customer that you've discovered this condition and tell them you'll research it further to determine its impacts.

C. Inform your customer that there is no problem with the additive except for an extremely small percentage of the population and release the product to them.

D. Tell the customer you'll correct the reaction problems in the next batch, but you'll release the first batch of product to them now to begin using.

83. You are a project manager working on gathering requirements and establishing estimates for the project. Which process group are you in?

A. Planning

B. Executing

C. Initiating

D. Monitoring and Controlling

84. According to the PMBOK® Guide, which of the following names all the components of an interactive communication model?

A. Encode, transmit, decode

B. Encode, transmit, decode, acknowledge, feedback/response

C. Encode, transmit, decode, feedback/response

D. Encode, transmit, acknowledge, decode

85. Who is responsible for performing and managing project integration when using an agile project management approach?

A. Team members

B. Product owner

C. Scrum master

D. Project manager

86. The Plan Procurement process applies evaluation criteria to bids and proposals and selects a vendor. It also uses independent estimates to compare vendor prices. This is also known as which of the following?

A. Independent comparisons

B. Analytical techniques

C. Should cost estimates

D. Expert judgment

87. All of the following statements are true of the project Closing process group except for which one?

A. Probability for success is greatest in the project Closing process group.

B. The project manager's influence is greatest in the project Closing process group.

C. The stakeholders' influence is least in the project Closing process group.

D. Risk occurrence is greatest in the project Closing process group.

88. Which of the following can you use in addition to the probability and impact matrix to prioritize risks?

A. Urgency

B. Manageability

C. Propinquity

D. Detectability

E. PESTLE

F. A, B, C, D

G. A, B, C, D, E

89. As a PMP® credential holder, one of your responsibilities is to ensure integrity on the project. When your personal interests are put above the interests of the project or when you use your influence to cause others to make decisions in your favor without regard for the project outcome, this is considered which of the following?

A. Conflict of interest

B. Using professional knowledge inappropriately

C. Culturally unacceptable

D. Personal conflict issue

89. Which organization has set the de facto standards for project management principles, processes, and techniques?

A. PMBOK®

B. PMO

C. PMI®

D. PBO

90. You work for a textile manufacturing firm. Your organization is introducing a new color line for their drapery materials. Changing colors for these materials during the manufacturing

process is straightforward. This is considered which of the following?

A. Project initiation
B. Ongoing operations
C. A project
D. Project execution

91. Your company manufactures small kitchen appliances. It is introducing a new product line of appliances in designer colors with distinctive features for kitchens in small spaces. These new products will be offered indefinitely starting with the spring catalog release. Which of the following is true?

A. This is a project because this new product line has never been manufactured and sold by this company before.

B. This is an ongoing operation because the company is in the business of manufacturing kitchen appliances. Introducing designer colors and features is simply a new twist on an existing process.

C. This is an ongoing operation because the new product line will be sold indefinitely. It's not temporary.

D. This is not a project or an ongoing operation. This is a new product introduction not affecting ongoing operations.

92. Your company manufactures small kitchen appliances. It is introducing a new product line of appliances in designer colors with distinctive features for kitchens in small spaces. This project was approved by the stakeholders and you have been appointed the project manager. These new products will be offered starting with the spring online release. To determine the characteristics and features of the new product line, you will have to perform which of the following? (Choose two.)

A. Defining business value for the new product line

B. Consulting with the stakeholders about the characteristics and features of the new product line

C. Planning the project life cycle for the project

D. Progressively elaborating the characteristics and features of the new product line

93. You've been hired as a manager for the adjustments department of a nationwide bank based in your city. The adjustments department is responsible

for making corrections to customer accounts. This is a large department, with several smaller sections that deal with specific accounts, such as personal checking or commercial checking. You've received your first set of management reports and can't make heads or tails of the information. Each section appears to use a different methodology to audit their work and record the data for the management report. You request that a project manager from the PMO come down and get started right away on a project to streamline this process and make the data and reports consistent. This project came about as a result of which of the following?

A. Technological advance
B. Organizational need
C. Customer request
D. Legal requirement

94. Which of the following applies a set of tools and techniques used to describe, organize, and monitor the work of project activities to meet the project requirements?

A. Project managers
B. The PMBOK® Guide
C. Project management
D. Stakeholders

95. Which of the following are true regarding multiphased relationships? (Choose three.)

A. Planning for an iterative phase begins while the work of other phases is progressing.
B. Overlapping phases occur when more than one phase is being performed at the same time.
C. During sequentially phased projects, the previous phase must finish before the next phase can begin.
D. Phase reviews should occur at the end of every phase.

96. Agile project life cycle methodologies are characterized by which of the following? (Choose three.)

A. Dividing tasks into small deliverables that can be completed in a short time frame.
B. Using a step-by-step process where one task is completed followed by another.
C. This methodology is used primarily in the software development industry but can be applied across other industry areas.
D. This methodology allows the project team to quickly adapt to new requirements and receive continuous feedback.

97. Your company sells Internet of Things appliances. They've just learned that another company is going to offer the same appliances

you offer with new, updated features and functionality. Your project came about to incorporate similar features in your product line. What is the business reason or need that brought this project about?

A. Technological advance
B. Competitive forces
C. Market demand
D. Business process improvements

98. All of the following statements are true except for which one?

A. Programs are groups of related projects.
B. Project life cycles are collections of sequential, iterative, and overlapping project phases.
C. A project may or may not be part of a program.
D. Portfolios are collections of interdependent projects or programs.

99. What are the five project management process groups, in order?

A. Initiating, Executing, Planning, Monitoring and Controlling, and Closing
B. Initiating, Monitoring and Controlling, Planning, Executing, and Closing
C. Initiating, Planning, Monitoring and Controlling, Executing, and Closing

D. Initiating, Planning, Executing, Monitoring and Controlling, and Closing

100. During which project management process group are risk and stakeholders' ability to influence project outcomes the highest?

A. Planning
B. Executing
C. Initiating
D. Monitoring and Controlling

101. Which of the following are true about a PMO? (Choose three.)

A. There are three types of PMOs: supportive, controlling, and collaborative.
B. The PMO is often responsible for implementing the OPM.
C. The key purpose of the PMO is to provide support to project managers.
D. The PMO facilitates communication within and across projects.

102. Which of the following agile methodologies describes the seven wastes?

A. Scrum
B. Six Sigma
C. Kaizen
D. Kanban

103.　Which of the following agile methodologies are a type of pull system? (Choose two.)

A. Kaizen
B. Six Sigma
C. Lean
D. XP
E. Scrum
F. Kanban

104.　Which of the following agile methodologies relies heavily on statistical data?

A. Kaizen
B. Six Sigma
C. Lean
D. XP
E. Scrum
F. Kanban

105.　Which of the following are characteristics of a predictive methodology? (Choose three.)

A. The results of the work of the project are often not delivered until the end of the project.
B. This methodology requires continuous feedback from your stakeholders throughout the project.
C. Changes to the project require a review of project plans and documenting the changes in the project plan.
D. Predictive methodologies might use a phased approach where deliverables are produced at the end of each phase.
E. The project team reviews the work of the project with the stakeholders in an iterative fashion so that they can incorporate modifications to functionality in the next phase.

106.　Which of the following are true regarding the Agile Manifesto? (Choose two.)

A. It is concerned with the quality of the deliverable.
B. Success is measured in incremental steps.
C. The focus is on the value to the customer.
D. It measures how efficiently the process was performed.
E. It is concerned with business process improvements.

107.　Match the following terms with the statements that describe them.

Term Description
A. Project and program management
1. Concerned with working on the right projects at the right time
B. Portfolio management
2. Centralized unit that oversees the management of projects throughout the organization
C. Organization project management
3. Focus on performing the projects in the right way

D. Project management office
4. Ensures projects are aligned with the organization's strategic business objectives

108. Your project team has a solid idea of the requirements for the project up front. Some specific elements of the deliverables are known at this point. Not all deliverables have been completely defined yet. The team would like to start with the known requirements and specific deliverables and then change their approach later in the development phase to incrementally deliver results. What development life cycle does this describe?

A. Incremental
B. Predictive
C. Hybrid
D. Agile

109. Which of the following statements is not true regarding EEFs and OPAs?

A. OPAs are external to the organization.
B. EEFs are outside the control of the project team.
C. Resource availability is an example of internal EEF.
D. Change control processes are an example of an OPA.
E. EEFs may drive compliance requirements on the project.

110. Which of the following is true regarding the project charter? (Choose two.)

A. The project charter should be issued by a manager external to the project.
B. The project charter is not created when you are using a hybrid life-cycle methodology.
C. The project charter should be issued by the project manager.
D. The project charter should be issued by the project sponsor.
E. The project charter assists the project manager in setting a clear vision and mission for the project and aligns stakeholder needs and expectations with the project objectives.

111. The Integration Knowledge Area is highly interactive and may involve iteratively performing the Planning, Executing, and Monitoring and Controlling processes. Which of the following is true regarding this Knowledge Area? (Choose two.)

A. Integration is managed and performed by the agile team when using an adaptive project management methodology.
B. The project manager determines which project management processes will interact with one another and integrates them appropriately.

C. Performing integration is a critical skill all project managers should possess.

D. Integration can be iterative and focuses on ensuring the schedule is defined, communication is planned and managed, and risks are continually identified.

E. Integration is only used with predictive project management methodologies.

112.   You are the project manager for Fun Days Vacation Resorts. Your new project assignment is to head up the Fun Days resort opening in Austin, Texas. First, you estimate the duration of the project management plan activities. When that activity is complete, you start devising the project schedule, and once the work has started, you will follow the process involved with monitoring and controlling deviations from the schedule. Which of the following is true regarding this question? (Choose two.)

A. This describes the Project Integration Management Knowledge Area.

B. This describes a predictive project management methodology.

C. This describes the Project Scope Management Knowledge Area.

D. This describes the Project Schedule Management Knowledge Area.

E. This describes an agile project management methodology.

113.   Which of the following is not true about the benefits management plan?

A. It is created early in the project and is reviewed at each phase gate.

B. It documents the expected benefits the project will bring about and how the benefits will be measured.

C. It is an important input to the Develop Project Charter process and helps to define a clear vision and mission for the project.

D. It creates strategic alignment of benefits to the organizational goals.

E. It assigns benefit owners to monitor benefit realization.

114.   According to the PMBOK® Guide, all of the following are elements of a business case except for which one?

A. The findings from the feasibility study are documented in the business case.

B. It is preceded by a needs assessment, which will assess the needs and demands of the project, costs, risk, and opportunities.

C. It names the project manager.

D. It must be approved before proceeding with the project.

115. Your nonprofit organization is preparing to host its first annual 5K run/walk in City Park. You worked on a similar project for the organization two years ago when it cohosted the 10K run through Overland Pass. Which of the organizational process assets might be most helpful to you on your new project?

A. The organization's marketing plans

B. Historical information from a previous project

C. The marketplace and political conditions

D. The organization's project management information systems

116. When using an agile methodology to manage your project, all of the following Knowledge Areas have processes that are performed before, during, and after an iteration except for which one?

A. Risk Management

B. Schedule Management

C. Procurement Management

D. Quality Management

117. You need to collaborate with the stakeholders to determine project approval requirements. Which of the following describes project approval requirements?

A. This describes what constitutes project success and how it will be measured.

B. This describes the conditions that must be met in order to close the project.

C. This is used in agile project management to determine if an iteration is successful.

D. This is determined by the project manager in the project charter.

118. You are the project manager for the Late Night Smooth Jazz Club chain, with stores in 12 states. Smooth Jazz is considering opening a new club in Arizona or Nevada. You have derived the following information:

Project Arizona: The payback period is 18 months, and the NPV is (250).

Project Nevada: The payback period is 24 months, and the NPV is 300.

Which project would you recommend to the selection committee?

A. Project Arizona, because the payback period is shorter than the payback period for Project Nevada

B. Project Nevada, because its NPV is a positive number

C. Project Arizona, because its NPV is a negative number

D. Project Nevada, because its NPV is a higher number than Project Arizona's NPV

119.   You are the project manager for the Late Night Smooth Jazz Club chain, with stores in 12 states. Smooth Jazz is considering opening a new club in Kansas City or Spokane. You have derived the following information:

Project Kansas City: The payback period is 27 months, and the IRR is 6 percent.

Project Spokane: The payback period is 25 months, and the IRR is 5 percent.

Which project should you recommend to the selection committee?

A. Project Spokane, because the payback period is the shortest

B. Project Kansas City, because the payback period is the longest

C. Project Spokane, because the IRR is the lowest

D. Project Kansas City, because the IRR is the highest

120.   Which of the following is true regarding NPV?

A. NPV assumes reinvestment at the cost of capital.

B. NPV decisions should be made based on the lowest value for all the selections.

C. NPV assumes reinvestment at the prevailing rate.

D. NPV assumes reinvestment at the NPV rate.

121.   You are the project manager for Insomniacs International. Since you don't sleep much, you get a lot of project work done. You're considering recommending a project that costs $575,000; expected inflows are $25,000 per quarter for the first two years and then $75,000 per quarter thereafter.

What is the payback period?

A. 40 months

B. 38 months

C. 39 months

D. 41 months

122.   Which of the following is true regarding IRR?

A. IRR assumes reinvestment at the cost of capital.

B. IRR is not difficult to calculate.

C. IRR is a constrained optimization method.

D. IRR is the discount rate when NPV is equal to zero.

123.   Which of the following is not true regarding the purpose of a business case?

A. It is an economic feasibility study that helps determine whether the investment in the project is worthwhile.

B. It describes the need or demand that brought about the project.

C. It describes how the benefits of the project will be measured and obtained.

D. It contains the results of the benefit measurement methods that will assist in project selection.

124. Which of the following is true regarding stakeholders and the project charter? (Choose three.)

A. The project charter will be used to ensure that stakeholders' expectations are in alignment with the project scope and with the final results of the project.

B. The results of the needs assessment are documented in the project charter so that stakeholders' expectations are in alignment with the project scope and with the final results of the project.

C. The project charter documents the stakeholders who will own monitoring and measuring the benefits of the project to ensure they are realized.

D. The project charter will be aligned with other project planning documents created later in the project, and this will ensure that the stakeholders understand the project objectives.

E. The Develop Project Charter process resides in the Project Stakeholder Management Knowledge Area process because this Knowledge Area is concerned that stakeholders' expectations are in alignment with the project scope and with the final results of the project.

F. The project manager is responsible for informing the stakeholders that the project charter has been approved and ensuring that they receive a copy.

125. Your selection committee is debating between two projects. Project A has a payback period of 18 months. Project B has a cost of $125,000, with expected cash inflows of $50,000 the first year and $25,000 per quarter after that.

Which project should you recommend?

A. Either Project A or Project B, because the payback periods are equal

B. Project A, because Project B's payback period is 21 months

C. Project A, because Project B's payback period is 24 months

D. Project A, because Project B's payback period is 20 months

126. Which of the following is true?

A. Discounted cash flow analysis is the least precise of the cash flow techniques because it does not consider the time value of money.

B. NPV is the least precise of the cash flow analysis techniques because it assumes reinvestment at the discount rate.

C. Payback period is the least precise of the cash flow analysis techniques because it does not consider the time value of money.

D. IRR is the least precise of the cash flow analysis techniques because it assumes reinvestment at the cost of capital.

127.   You are a project manager for Zippy Tees. Your selection committee has just chosen a project you recommended for implementation. Your project is to manufacture a line of miniature stuffed bears that will be attached to your company's trendy T-shirts. The bears will be wearing the same T-shirt design as the shirt to which they're attached. Your project sponsor thinks you've impressed the big boss and wants you to skip to the manufacturing process right away. What is your response?

A. Agree with the project sponsor because that person is your boss and has a lot of authority and power in the company.

B. Require that a preliminary budget be established and a resource list be put together to alert other managers of the requirements of this project.

This should be published and signed by the other managers who are impacted by this project.

C. Require that a project charter be written and signed off on by all stakeholders before proceeding.

D. Suggest that a preliminary business case be written to outline the objectives of the project.

128.   Which of the following state the four main components of maintaining project artifacts?

A. Ensuring that documents are stored appropriately

B. Ensuring that documents are easily accessible to stakeholders

C. Ensuring that documents are kept up to date with versioning control

D. Ensuring that documents are printed and stored in a project notebook(s) for future reference

E. Ensuring that documents and artifacts are distributed appropriately

129.   A project is considered successful when _____.

A. the product of the project has been manufactured.

B. the project sponsor announces the completion of the project.

C. the product of the project is turned over to the operations area to handle the ongoing aspects of the project.

D. the project achieves its objectives and meets the expectations of the stakeholders.

130. The VP of customer service has expressed concern over a project in which you're involved. His specific concern is that if the project is implemented as planned, he'll have to purchase additional equipment to staff his customer service center. The cost was not taken into consideration in the project budget. The project sponsor insists that the project must go forward as originally planned or the customer will suffer.

Which of the following are true? (Choose two.)

A. The VP of customer service is correct. Since the cost was not taken into account at the beginning of the project, the project should not go forward as planned. Project initiation should be revisited to examine the project plan and determine how changes can be made to accommodate customer service.

B. The conflict should be resolved in favor of the customer.

C. Stakeholder identification should occur as early in the project as possible.

D. The conflict should be resolved in favor of the VP of customer service.

131. The amount of authority a project manager possesses can be related to which of the following? (Choose three.)

A. The organizational structure

B. The power and influence key stakeholders possess on the project

C. The interaction with various levels of management

D. The project management maturity level of the organization

E. The project management methodology you'll use to manage the project

132. Which of the following are true regarding functional organizations? (Choose three.)

A. All employees report to one manager and have a clear chain of command.

B. Organizational structures and culture are independent from the project management methodology you'll use to manage the project.

C. The organization is focused on projects and project work.

D. Teams are co-located.

E. Using adaptive and hybrid methodologies in this structure is possible but can be challenging.

133. You have completed the Develop Project Charter and Identify Stakeholder processes.

What phase does this relate to in the Six Sigma DMAIC methodology?

A. Analyze
B. Control
C. Measure
D. Define

134. It is important for a project manager to identify stakeholders and understand their needs, interests, and influence. All of the following are true regarding stakeholders in this context except which one?

A. Organizational structures and hierarchy, culture, geographic locations, global trends, and locations of resources and facilities can impact stakeholder power, influence, and interest on the project.

B. Stakeholders often have conflicting interests and the project manager needs to understand the conflicts in order to resolve them and manage stakeholder expectations.

C. Stakeholders may have the power and influence to cause issues on the project. You'll need to identify and assess them so that you know their needs and can address issues early in a way that keeps the stakeholders engaged.

D. The Identify Stakeholder process should be repeated often throughout the project.

E. All of the above.

135. You have performed variance analysis and discovered that you need to take action to get the project back on track. Which of the following are true? (Choose two.)

A. Corrections and changes due to variance analysis findings can be made quickly using an agile project management methodology.

B. Variance analysis compares the work performed to the project management baseline documents such as schedule, cost, and scope.

C. The project sponsor is responsible for ensuring corrective actions are taken to get the project back on track no matter which project management methodology you are using.

D. Change requests may bring about corrective actions.

136. The VP of customer service has expressed concern over a project you are managing. Her specific concern is that if the project is implemented as planned, she'll be missing an important feature enabling a call-back function where customers will not have to wait online but will receive a call back when they are next up in the queue. This functionality was not taken into consideration in the

project plan, and this new wrinkle will delay the project by two months. The business value for this project is improving customer satisfaction. Customer surveys show that satisfaction levels are low when it comes to wait times and overall call resolution time. The CEO was expecting this project to go live early in the fiscal year so that customer service scores would show an improvement, thereby increasing satisfaction along with making the board happy. Which of the following is true regarding this scenario?

A. This project was brought about due to customer requests.
B. Customer satisfaction surveys could be used to determine if the business value was met.
C. The project manager must champion the business value for this project.
D. The project manager should consider delivering business value incrementally by using an agile approach.
E. All of the above.

137.   Match the following categories associated with analyzing stakeholders in the Salience model with their classification.

Category	Classification
A. Legitimacy + urgency	1. Dangerous
B. Power	2. Dependent
C. Power + urgency	3. Dominant
D. Urgency	4. Dormant
E. Legitimacy	5. Discretionary
F. Power + legitimacy	6. Demanding

138.   Which term refers to those values that will lead to short- and long-term benefits for the organization?
A. Business process improvement
B. Business value
C. Continuous improvement

D. Value network

139.   You have identified, obtained contact information for, assessed, classified, and prioritized your stakeholders. Which of the following is true? (Choose three.)

A. You have documented this information in the stakeholder register.

B. You should use caution when making some of this information available to all project stakeholders.

C. You have used the power/interest grid to obtain this information.

D. You've analyzed influence, power, interest, impact, directions of influence, and power, urgency, and legitimacy as part of the tools and techniques of the Identify Stakeholder process.

140.   Match the following roles in the agile methodologies with their titles.

Role	Description
A. Product owner	1. The title similar to a project manager in the Lean methodology
B. Sensei	2. The title similar to a project manager in the Kanban methodology
C. Flow master	3. A Six Sigma title
D. Team facilitator	4. Also known as the Scrum master. Coordinates the work of the sprint
E. Black belt	5. The liaison between the Scrum master and the stakeholders in a Scrum methodology. Also known as the voice of the customer

141.   All of the following are examples of business value except which one?

A. Create a new car model that's never been offered before.

B. Implement a new accounting system.

C. Create goodwill.

D. Improve employee engagement.

E. A and B

142.   The VP of Human Resources has requested a new timekeeping project for their machine shop workers. The business value for this project is improving payroll accuracy. The workers are threatening a strike because of the antiquated system in place now. The current system has ancient time clocks that rarely work, causing the workers to revert to paper timecards. This creates multiple errors in overtime pay and shift differential pay. Which of the following is true regarding this scenario? (Choose three.)

A. The project sponsor is the one responsible for delivering the business value of this project.

B. Urgency is objective and is defined by the project sponsor.

C. The urgency to deliver this project is the potential of an impending strike.

D. The goals of the project must be met within the time frame outlined in the project plan in order to realize business value.

E. The project manager should examine business value creation and compare this to the project management documents, such as the project charter, to ensure that the goals of the project are met and the business value is realized.

143.   You are using an agile approach to deliver business value incrementally. What other elements of business value should you be focused on? (Choose two)

A. Examining business value throughout the project

B. Reporting on business value only at the end of the project

C. Accepting suggestions about delivering incremental business value and ensuring that business value is achieved when the project is complete

D. Discussing business value with the project sponsor, recording it in the project charter, and expecting project team members and stakeholders to refer to this periodically

144.   How will you know that business value is being achieved?

A. By observing the work product

B. By asking the project sponsor

C. By measuring business value using KPIs

D. By requiring the project team to report on business value

145.   Your project requires contract resources with specific subject matter expertise to deliver business value. All of the following are true except which one?

A. The contractor is a member of the business value network.

B. The business value network is made up of external resources such as contractors, subject matter experts, suppliers, and delivery services.
C. Members of the value network work together to bring about business value to their customer, their organization, the end-user customer, and stakeholders.
D. It is the project manager's responsibility to ensure that the contractor understands the business value the project was created to bring about.

146. You are using an agile project management methodology to deliver business value. During each iteration, you and the team members are breaking down tasks into tangible components that have enough features and functionality to allow the customer to examine value and provide feedback to the team. Which of the following are true regarding this question when using a Scrum methodology? (Choose two.)

A. The product owner will determine whether business value has been achieved.
B. The project team will manage and prioritize the product backlog and choose the user stories for the upcoming iteration that can be broken down to the minimum viable product.
C. The Scrum master will assist the team in breaking down the user stories and assign each team member tasks for the upcoming iteration.
D. You are creating the minimum viable product.

147. Which of the following is true regarding assisting the team in subdividing tasks into the minimum viable product?

A. Each iteration will produce enough features to examine business value.
B. Each iteration will provide an opportunity for feedback on future iterations.
C. The minimum viable product allows the customer to see or experience the business value that was created.
D. All the options are correct.

148. All of the following are true regarding supporting the team in subdividing tasks into
the minimum viable product except for which one?
A. Business value is delivered incrementally.
B. Adjustments or corrections can only be made at the end of the iteration.
C. This process is used in an agile project management methodology, allowing small, tangible results to be delivered at the end of each iteration.
D. Tasks can be completed quickly, tested, and shown to the customer in a short period of time.

149. You are a project manager for Laredo Pioneer's Traveling Rodeo Show. You're heading up a small project to promote a new line of souvenirs to be sold at the shows. You know that the purpose of the project scope management plan and requirements management plan provide which of the following? (Choose three.)

A. They help set a clear vision and mission for the project.

B. They are used to further elaborate the project charter, which contains a list of high-level requirements needed to satisfy stakeholder expectations before starting the project management plan.

C. They serve as an agreement between the project management team and the project customer to document and agree on the work of the project and what it will produce.

D. They are both used to plan and manage the scope of the project.

150. You are a project manager for Laredo Pioneer's Traveling Rodeo Show.

You're heading up a small project to promote a new line of souvenirs to be sold at the shows. You've held the kickoff meeting and are ready to begin creating the project management plan. You know that a kickoff meeting is important for which of the following reasons? (Choose three.)

A. It ensures that compliance and regulatory requirements are documented and discussed and will be included in the project scope statement.

B. It communicates the start of the project and informs stakeholders of the project objectives and the business value the project will bring about.

C. It ensures that a common understanding is established among stakeholders because the key milestones and key deliverables are identified.

D. It ensures that policies, procedures, and standards used in the organization have been considered and discussed.

E. It helps establish stakeholder engagement and commitment.

151. You are a project manager responsible for the construction of a new office complex. You are taking over for a project manager who recently left the company. The prior project manager completed the project scope statement and scope management plan for this project. In your interviews with some key team members, you conclude which of the following? (Choose two.)

A. The project scope statement assesses the stability of the project scope and outlines how scope will be verified and used to control changes. The team members know that project scope is measured against the product requirements and that the scope management plan is based on the approved project scope.

B. The scope management plan describes how project scope will be managed and controlled and how the WBS will be created and defined. They know that product scope is measured against the product requirements and that the scope management plan is based on the approved project scope.

C. The scope management plan is deliverables-oriented and includes cost estimates and stakeholder needs and expectations. They understand that project scope is measured against the project management plan and that the scope management plan is based on the approved project charter.

D. The project scope statement describes how the high-level deliverables and requirements will be defined and verified. They understand that product scope is measured against the project management plan and that the scope management plan is based on the approved project charter.

E. The project scope management plan defines, maintains, and manages the scope of the project.

152.   Unanimity, majority, plurality, and autocratic are four examples of which of the following techniques and what they are used for? (Choose two.)

A. They are used to help stakeholders come to conclusions and agreement on the requirements needed to fulfill the project objectives.

B. Interviews, which is a tool and technique of the Define Scope process.

C. Facilitated workshops technique, which is a tool and technique of the Define Scope process.

D. Decision-making techniques, which is a tool and technique of the Collect Requirements process.

E. They are used to help stakeholders visualize decisions using tools such as mind mapping or affinity diagrams.

153.   You are working on a project where the requirements and scope are well defined, but you know there will be changes when performing the work of the project. Your stakeholders will need to provide continuous feedback during the development stages of this project. Which of the following are true when determining the deliverables for the project?

(Choose three.)

A. You should use a predictive approach to manage this project. You will document a project scope statement because it describes how the team will define and develop the work breakdown structure.

B. You should use a hybrid approach for this project. Because the requirements and deliverables are well defined, you may choose to document a project scope statement that further elaborates the deliverables of the project and serves as a basis for future project decisions.

C. You should document the project scope statement so there is agreement between the project management team and the project customer and everyone knows what the work of the project will produce.

D. You may choose to document the project scope statement because it assesses the reliability of the project scope and describes the process for verifying and accepting completed deliverables.

E. You should use a hybrid approach for this project because the stakeholders would like to provide continuous feedback on the deliverables once the work of the project starts. User stories will be used to fulfill the deliverables of the project and will be pulled to the backlog.

154. You are a project manager for an agricultural supply company. You have interviewed stakeholders and gathered their project requirements in the Collect Requirements process. Which of the following is true regarding the process to which this question refers?

A. The requirements document lists the requirements and describes how they will be analyzed, documented, and managed throughout the project.

B. Requirements documentation consists of formal, complex documents that include elements such as the business need of the project, functional requirements, nonfunctional requirements, impacts to others inside and outside the organization, and requirements assumptions and constraints.

C. The requirements documentation details the work required to create the deliverables of the project, including deliverables description, product acceptance criteria, exclusions from requirements, and requirements assumptions and constraints.

D. The requirements traceability matrix ties requirements to project objectives, business needs, WBS deliverables, product design, test strategies, and high-level requirements and traces them through to project completion.

155. Which of the following makes up the scope baseline when using a predictive life-cycle approach?

A. The approved project scope statement
B. The approved scope management plan
C. The approved WBS
D. The approved WBS dictionary
E. A, B, C, D
F. A, C, D

156. Which of the following statements is true regarding brainstorming and lateral thinking? (Choose two.)

A. They are techniques that can be used in several Planning processes to help determine project scope, requirements, assumptions, constraints, and more.

B. Lateral thinking is a form of alternatives generation that's considered thinking outside the box.

C. They are decision-making techniques used to help stakeholders form consensus.

D. Brainstorming is a technique involving plurality decision-making.

157. Your company, Kick That Ball Sports, has appointed you as project manager for its new Cricket product line introduction. This is a national effort, and all the retail stores across the country need to have the new products on the shelves before the media advertising blitz begins. The product line involves three new products, two of which will be introduced together and a third one that will follow within two years. You are ready to create the WBS. All of the following are true except for which one?

A. The WBS may be structured using each product as a level one entry.

B. The WBS should be elaborated to a level where costs and schedule are easily estimated. This is known as the work package level.

C. Rolling wave refers to how all levels of the WBS collectively roll up to reflect the work of the project and only the work of the project.

D. Each level of the WBS represents verifiable products or results.

158. You are a project manager for Giraffe Enterprises. You've recently taken over for a project manager who lied about his PMI® certification and was subsequently fired. Unfortunately, he did a poor job of defining the project scope. The project scope statement is the last document the previous project manager created. You will need to create the remaining subsidiary project management plans and documents. All of the following could happen if you don't correct this except for which one?

A. The stakeholders will require overtime from the project team to keep the project on schedule.

B. The poor scope definition will adversely affect the creation of the work breakdown structure, and costs may increase.

C. The project scope statement is used to document the process for defining, maintaining, and managing project scope.

D. The project costs could increase, there might be rework, and schedule delays might result.

159. You are the project manager for Lucky Stars nightclubs. They specialize in live country and western band performances. Your newest

project is in the Planning process group. You are working on the WBS. The finance manager has given you a numbering system to assign to the WBS. Which of the following is true?

A. The numbering system is a unique identifier known as the WBS dictionary, which is used to assign quality control codes to the individual work elements.

B. The numbering system is a unique identifier known as the WBS dictionary, which is used to track the descriptions of individual work elements.

C. The numbering system is a unique identifier known as the control account, which is used to track time and resource assignments for individual work elements.

D. The numbering system is a unique identifier known as the code of accounts identifier, which is used to track the costs of the WBS elements.

160.   You are a project manager working on a large, complex project. You've constructed the WBS for this project, and all of the work package levels are subprojects of this project. You've requested that the subproject managers report to you in three weeks with their individual WBSs constructed. Which of the following statements are correct? (Choose three.)

A. The work package level is decomposed to create the activity list.

B. The work package level is the lowest level in the WBS and is known as a user story on an agile project.

C. The work package level facilitates resource assignments.

D. The work package level facilitates cost and time estimates.

161.   You are a project manager working on a new software product your company plans to market to businesses. The project sponsor told you that the project must be completed by September 1. The company plans to demo the new software product at a trade show in late September and, therefore, needs the project completed in time for the trade show. However, the sponsor has also told you that the budget is fixed at $85,000, and it would take an act of Congress to get it increased. You must complete the project within the given time frame and budget. Which of the following is the primary constraint for this project?

A. Budget
B. Scope
C. Time
D. Quality

162.   Which of the following statements about decomposition is true?

A. Decomposition is a five-step process used to break down the work of the project.

B. Decomposition requires expert judgment along with close analysis of the project scope statement.

C. Decomposition is a tool and technique used to create a WBS and subdivide the major deliverables into smaller components until the work package level is reached.

D. Decomposition is used in the agile methodology to create users stories at the work package level. They are documented in the product backlog and pulled from here into the iteration backlog at the beginning of each iteration.

E. All of the above.

163. You are documenting acceptance criteria for your deliverables. Which of the following are true? (Choose two.)

A. They are documented in the project scope management plan in a predictive methodology.

B. They are not used in an adaptive methodology because the work is defined at the beginning of the iteration and verified at the end of the iteration.

C. They are used in a predictive methodology to test or measure whether the deliverables of the project are acceptable and satisfactory when the deliverables are completed.

D. They are documented in user stories in an adaptive methodology to test or measure whether the deliverables of the project are acceptable and satisfactory at the end of the iteration.

164. You are a project manager for a documentary film company. The company president wants to produce a new documentary on the efforts of heroic rescue teams and get it on air as soon as possible. She's looking to you to make this documentary the best that has ever been produced in the history of this company. She guarantees you free rein to use whatever resources you need to get this project done quickly. However, the best photographer in the company is currently working on another assignment. Which of the following is true?

A. The primary constraint is time because the president wants the film done quickly. She told you to get it to air as soon as possible.

B. Resources are the primary constraint. Even though the president has given you free rein on resource use, you assume she didn't mean those actively assigned to projects.

C. The schedule is the primary constraint. Even though the president has given you free rein on resource use, you assume she didn't mean those actively assigned to projects. The photographer won't be finished for another three weeks on his current assignment, so schedule adjustments will have to be made.

D. The primary constraint is quality because the president wants this to be the best film ever produced by this company. She's given you free rein to use whatever resources are needed to get the job done.

165.   Your project depends on a key deliverable from a vendor you've used several times before with great success. You're counting on the delivery to arrive on June 1. This is an example of a/an

_____.

A. Constraint
B. Objective
C. Assumption
D. Requirement

166.   You are creating your project management plan. The project you are working on involves accepting credit cards on your organization's website. This will require yearly audits to ensure you are following best practices in developing your website and not exposing sensitive customer information. Which of the following EEFs should you consider given this scenario? (Choose two.)

A. Technology issue
B. Regulatory standard
C. Compliance issue
D. Constraint

167.   Your company provides answering services for several major catalog retailers. The number of calls coming into the service center per month has continued to increase over the past 18 months. The phone system is approaching the maximum load limits and needs to be upgraded. You've been assigned to head up the upgrade project. Based on the company's experience with the vendor who worked on the last phone upgrade project, you're confident they'll be able to assist you with this project as well. Which of the following is true?

A. You've made an assumption about vendor availability and expertise. The project came about because of a business need.

B. Vendor availability and expertise are constraints. The project came about because of a business need.

C. You've made an assumption about vendor availability and expertise. The project came about because of a market demand.

D. Vendor availability and expertise are constraints. The project came about because of a market demand.

168.   Which of the following is not a major step of decomposition?
A. Identify major deliverables.
B. Identify resources.
C. Identify components.
D. Verify correctness of decomposition

169.   You are the project manager for Changing Tides video games. You are in the process of breaking the work packages into activities. Which of the following options are true? (Choose two.)
A. When using an agile methodology, activity lists are created using only the tools and techniques of the Define Activities process.
B. The iteration planning meeting is the only time that activities are identified and estimated when using an agile methodology.
C. You can use rolling wave planning, a form of progressive elaboration, to help create activity lists in both predictive and adaptive methodologies.
D. User stories are chosen by the product owner at the iteration planning meeting and the team members break them down into activities for the iteration.

170.   You are the project manager for Changing Tides video games. Your project is a bit ambiguous at first. It's similar in complexity and magnitude to a project that the team members worked on last year. The key stakeholder wants to be actively involved and be able to modify the requirements as the project progresses. The team is ready to define and estimate activities. Which of the following statements are true? (Choose three.)
A. You should use an agile methodology to deliver business value incrementally and accommodate the need for changes to the requirements.
B. You should use an agile methodology, and the schedule management plan is not needed with this approach.
C. When using an agile methodology, there is a maximum focus on value to the customer and minimal focus on process.
D. Backlog items are prioritized based on business need, risk, and value to the organization. The most important user stories are at the top of the backlog list.

171.   Your project's primary constraint is quality. To make certain the project team members don't feel too pressed for time and to avoid

schedule risk, you decide to use which of the following activity estimating tools?

A. Three-point estimates
B. Analogous estimating
C. Reserve analysis
D. Parametric estimating

172. You have been hired as a contract project manager for Grapevine Vineyards. Grapevine wants you to design an Internet wine club for its customers. One of the activities for this project is the installation and testing of several new servers. You know from past experience it takes about 16 hours per server to accomplish this task. Since you're installing 10 new servers, you estimate this activity to take 160 hours. Which of the estimating techniques have you used?

A. Parametric estimating
B. Analogous estimating
C. Bottom-up estimating
D. Reserve analysis

173. Which of the following statements describe the activity list? (Choose three.)

A. The activity list is an output of the Define Activities process.
B. The activity list includes all activities of the project.
C. The activity list is an extension of and a component of the WBS.
D. The activity list includes an identifier and description of the activity.

174. You have been hired as a contract project manager for Grapevine Vineyards. Grapevine wants you to design an Internet wine club for its customers. Customers must register before being allowed to order wine over the Internet so that legal age can be established. You know that the module to verify registration must be written and tested using data from Grapevine's existing database. This new module cannot be tested until the data from the existing system is loaded. This is an example of which of the following?

A. Preferential logic
B. Soft logic
C. Discretionary dependency
D. Hard logic

175.   Match the following values from the Agile Manifesto.Table of Agile Manifesto Principles

Values this	Over this
A. Responding to change	1. Contract negotiation
B. Working software	2. Following a plan
C. Customer collaboration	3. Process and tools
D. Individuals and interactions	4. Comprehensive documentation

176.   You are working on a project that requires resources with expertise in the areas of hospitality management and entertainment. You have prepared the project schedule and notified the functional managers about the resources you'll need, and when, from their areas. What are the other things you should do?

A. Make the schedule available to stakeholders by posting it to the project site so that it is accessible to them.

B. Be certain to notify stakeholders of any schedule updates or changes.

C. Save a schedule baseline for comparative purposes in case changes are made to the baseline.

D. All of the above.

177.   Which logical relationship does the PDM use most often?

A. Start-to-finish

B. Start-to-start

C. Finish-to-finish

D. Finish-to-start

178.   You are a project manager for Picture Shades, Inc. Your company manufactures window shades that have replicas of Renaissance-era paintings for hotel chains. Picture Shades is taking its product to the home market, and you're managing the new project. It will offer its products at retail stores as well as on its website. You're developing the project schedule for this undertaking and have determined the critical path. Which of the following statements is true?

A. You calculated the most likely start date and most likely finish date, float time, and weighted average estimates.

B. You calculated the activity dependency and the optimistic and pessimistic activity duration estimates.

C. You calculated the early and late start dates, the early and late finish dates, and float times for all activities.

D. You calculated the optimistic, pessimistic, and most likely duration times and the float times for all activities.

179.   You are a project manager for Picture Shades, Inc. Your company manufactures window shades that have replicas of Renaissance-era paintings for hotel chains. Picture Shades is taking its product to the home market, and you're managing the new project. It will offer its products at retail stores as well as on its website. You're developing the project schedule for this undertaking. Looking at the following graph, which path is the critical path?

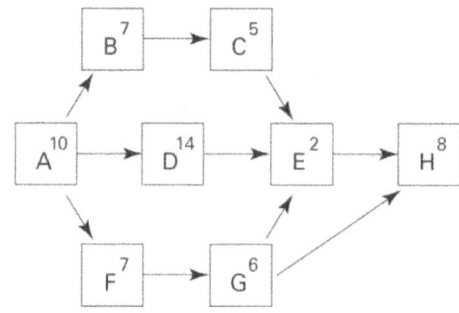

A. A-B-C-E-H
B. A-D-E-H
C. A-F-G-H
D. A-F-G-E-H

180.   Use the following graphic to answer this question. If the duration of activity B was changed to 10 days and the duration of activity G was changed to 9 days, which path is the critical path?

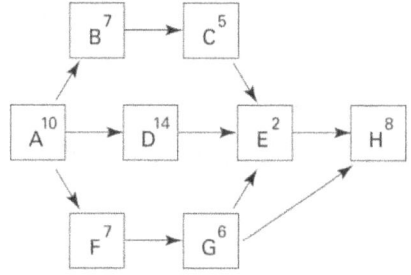

A. A-B-C-E-H
B. A-D-E-H
C. A-F-G-H
D. A-F-G-E-H

181. Which of the following statements is true regarding the critical path?

A. It should not be compressed.
B. It allows for looping and branching.
C. The critical path technique is the same as PERT.
D. It's the duration of all tasks with zero or negative float.

182. You are a project manager for Move It Now trucking company. Your company specializes in moving household goods across the city or across the country. Your project involves upgrading the nationwide computer network for the company. Your lead engineer has given you the following estimates for a critical path activity: 60 days most likely, 72 days pessimistic, 48 days optimistic. What is the weighted average or expected value?

A. 54
B. 66
C. 60
D. 30

183. You are a project manager for Move It Now trucking company. Your company specializes in moving household goods across the city or across the country. Your project involves upgrading the nationwide computer network for the company. Your lead engineer has given you the following estimates for a critical path activity: 60 days most likely, 72 days pessimistic, 48 days optimistic. What is the standard deviation?

A. 22
B. 20
C. 2
D. 4

184. If you know the expected value is 500 and the standard deviation is 12, you can say with approximately a 95 percent confidence rating which of the following?

A. The activity will take from 488 to 512 days.
B. The activity will take from 464 to 536 days.

C. The activity will take from 494 to 506 days.

D. The activity will take from 476 to 524 days.

185. This contains all the supporting detail regarding activity estimates and includes assumptions, the methods used to derive the estimates, constraints, resources used to develop the estimates, confidence levels, and risks.

A. Contingency estimates

B. Basis of estimates

C. Reserve estimates

D. Buffer estimates

186. You are the project manager working on a research project for a new drug treatment. Your preliminary project schedule runs past the due date for a federal grant application. The manager of the R&D department has agreed to release two resources to work on your project to meet the federal grant application date. This is an example of _____.

A. Crashing

B. Fast tracking

C. Resource leveling

D. Adjusting the resource calendar

187. You are the project manager for Rivera Gourmet Adventure Vacations. Rivera combines the wonderful tastes of great gourmet food with outdoor adventure activities. Your project involves installing a new human resources software system. Your stakeholders understand this is a large undertaking and that you might experience some schedule slippage. Jason, the database analyst working on this project, is overallocated. He is critical to the success of the project, and you don't want to burn him out by overscheduling him. Which of the following actions should you take?

A. You should use fast tracking to smooth out resource overallocation.

B. You should use crashing to resource level the critical path tasks.

C. You should use resource leveling to balance out resource assignments.

D. You should use resource smoothing to smooth out resource assignments.

188. Your Scrum team's velocity rate is 24 story points per iteration. There are 165 total story points. Which of the following statements are true regarding this question? (Choose two.)

A. Velocity is used to estimate the capacity of the Scrum team.
B. This information can be tracked on a burndown chart.
C. The project needs seven iterations to complete all of the work of the project.
D. A Kanban board can display this information.

189. Which of the following are true regarding the stakeholder engagement plan? (Choose two.)

A. The stakeholder engagement plan helps to define and manage the flow of information to the stakeholders.
B. The stakeholder engagement plan is developed by analyzing the needs, interests, and potential impacts of the stakeholders. It documents strategies needed to promote stakeholder decisionmaking and execution.
C. The stakeholder engagement plan captures the strategies needed to engage stakeholders throughout the project.
D. The stakeholder engagement plan documents the types of information needs the stakeholders have, when the information should be distributed, and how the information will be delivered.
E. The stakeholder engagement plan considers the organizational structure and stakeholder requirements.

190. When you're creating the cost management plan, which project elements should you consider and review? (Choose two.)

A. The approved project charter and project scope
B. The level of precision and accuracy
C. The units of measure and control thresholds
D. The project schedule and project resources

191. You are a project manager working for iTrim Central. Your organization has developed a new dieting technique that is sure to be the next craze. You're preparing your cost management plan. You know that all of the following are true regarding this plan except for which one?

A. The WBS provides the framework for this plan.
B. Units of measure should be described in the plan usually as hours, days, weeks, or lump sum.
C. This plan is a subsidiary of the project management plan.

D. Control thresholds should be described in the plan as to how estimates will adhere to rounding ($100 or $1,000, and so on).

192. You are a project manager working for iTrim Central. Yourorganization has developed a new dieting technique that is sure to be the next craze. One of the deliverables of your feasibility study was an analysis of the potential financial performance of this new product, and your executives are very pleased with the numbers. You will be working with several vendors to produce products, marketing campaigns, and software that will track customers' progress with the new techniques. For purposes of performing earned value measurements for project costs, you are going to place which of the following in the WBS?

A. Chart of accounts
B. Code of accounts
C. Control account
D. Reserve account

193. Which of the following options is the key component of determining cost estimates and should be completed as early in the project as possible?

A. Scope definition
B. Resource requirements
C. Activity cost estimates
D. Basis of estimates

194. You want to improve your cost estimates by taking into account estimation uncertainty and risk. Which of the following estimating techniques will you use?

A. Analogous estimates
B. Three-point estimating
C. Parametric estimates
D. Bottom-up estimates

195. When an agile team is communicating, several meetings occur including a daily stand-up. Which of the following options are true regarding the daily stand-up in an agile methodology? (Choose two.)

A. Stand-ups are intended to examine the work of the project and note corrections that are needed for the next iteration.
B. Iteration-based stand-ups focus on team members.

C. Stand-ups are intended to examine what is going well, and not so well, with the iteration.

D. Flow-based stand-ups focus on team capacity and workflow.

196.   Your organization has historically performed projects using a predictive methodology. You'd like to give the agile process a try. You have a low-risk, low-priority project that is perfect for this experiment. However, the project sponsor of this project is nervous about using a new approach that's never been tried before. Which of the following actions should you take in this scenario?

A. Make certain you are allocating time to mentoring stakeholders.

B. Ensure that the sponsor is committed to the project and to the methodology.

C. Mentor the sponsor and the stakeholders on the agile process by providing training to educate them on the agile processes.

D. Consider using a hybrid approach to help the sponsor feel a little more at ease, because this will mix some of the processes with which they are familiar with agile processes.

E. All of the above.

197.   You are the project manager for a custom home–building construction company. You are working on the model home project for the upcoming Homes Tour. The model home includes smart home connections, talking appliances, and wiring for home theaters. You are working on the cost baseline for this project. Which of the following statements are true? (Choose three.)

A. This process aggregates the estimated costs of project activities.

B. The cost baseline will be used to measure variances and future project performance.

C. This process assigns cost estimates for expected future period operating costs.

D. The cost baseline is the time-phased budget at completion for the project.

198.   Adaptive methodologies focus on eliminating waste, Lean thinking, and pull-based systems. When using this methodology, stakeholders are highly engaged with the project. Which of the following are true regarding positive stakeholder engagement in an adaptive methodology? (Choose three.)

A. Their engagement and the methodology creates transparency on the project.

B. Stakeholders have a neutral classification in an adaptive methodology.

C. Stakeholders have a supportive classification in an adaptive methodology.

D. Their engagement increases trust and reduces risk, increasing the changes for a successful project.

E. Stakeholders have a resistant classification when using an adaptive methodology.

199. You are the project manager for a custom home–building construction company. You are working on the model home project for the upcoming Homes Tour. The model home includes smart home connections, talking appliances, and wiring for home theaters. You are working on the Determine Budget process. Which of the following statements are true? (Choose three.)

A. You document the funding limit reconciliation to include a contingency for unplanned risks.

B. You discover that updates to the risk register are needed as a result of performing this process.

C. You document that funding requirements are derived from the cost baseline.

D. The performance measurement baseline will be used to perform earned value management calculations.

200. Which of the following is displayed as an S curve?

A. Funding requirements

B. Cost baseline

C. Cost estimates

D. Expenditures to date

Exam Answers

1. F. All of the options are considered when examining whether the tailoring processes and project integration management produced the results you were expecting.

2. D. Fast tracking is the best answer in this scenario. Budget was the original constraint on this project, so it's unlikely the project manager would get more resources to assist with the project. The next best thing is to compress phases to shorten the project duration.

3. A. Discretionary dependencies can create arbitrary total float values, and they can also limit scheduling options.

4. A. Project managers spend about 90 percent of their time communicating through status meetings, team meetings, email, verbal communications, and so on.

5. 5. A-6, B-7, C-4, D-3, E-1, F-5, G-2. Agile measurements should focus on customer value.

6. D. This question describes a predictive life cycle methodology. Options B, C, and D are all adaptive methodologies, which have high degrees of uncertainty, high risk, evolving requirements, and cross-functional teams.

7. A. Change control systems are a subset of the configuration management system. Change control systems manage changes to the deliverables and/or project baselines.

8. D The iterative approach uses prototypes and mockups produced in time-bound periods such as sprints. The incremental approach produces usable deliverables at the end of the workflow, which helps in performing the work faster and speeds up the project. The incremental approach focuses on speed of delivery and the iterative approach focuses on learning optimization.

9. A. This question describes an agile life cycle methodology. Hybrid life cycles have some degree of uncertainty and risk, but not at the level the question describes. Option C and D describe predictive methodologies which have high degrees of certainty, firm requirements, and stable teams.

10. C. The smoothing technique (also known as accommodate) does not usually result in a permanent solution. The problem is downplayed to

make it seem less important than it is, which makes the problem tend to resurface later.

11. B. The components of the interactive communication model are encode, transmit, decode, acknowledge, and feedback/response. The basic communication model consists of the sender, message, and receiver elements.

12. B. Benefit measurement methods are project selection methods that use benefit cost ratio and other financial analysis to select projects.

13. B. This question describes the forcing technique because the project sponsor insisted on implementing their solution. The forcing technique occurs when one party forces a solution on others.

14. F. These factors, and others, may impact the organization and/or your project and you should continually monitor and review both the internal and external environment for changes that can impact the project.

15. C. The scope management plan outlines how project scope will be managed and how scope changes will be incorporated into the project.

16. E. Cause-and-effect diagrams—also called Ishikawa, fishbone diagrams, and why-why diagrams—show the relationship between the effects of problems and their causes. Kaoru Ishikawa developed cause-and-effect diagrams.

17. C. Negotiation, influencing, and business skills are all important for a project manager to possess. However, good communication skills are the most important skills a project manager can have.

18. E. Inspections are also called reviews, peer reviews, walkthrough, and audits.

19. A. Analogous estimating—also called top-down estimating—is a form of expert judgment. Analogous estimating can be used to estimate cost or time and considers historical information from previous, similar projects.

20. A. Project managers have the highest level of power and authority in a project-oriented organization. They also have high levels of power and authority in a strong matrix organization.

21. C. Plan Stakeholder Engagement is concerned with determining the engagement levels of the stakeholders, understanding their needs and interests, and understanding how they might impact the project or how the project may impact them.

22. C. Unknown risks might be threats or opportunities to the project, and the project manager should set aside contingency reserves to deal with them.

23. C. Sharing knowledge and creating knowledge are the focus of this process. Option A describes the Manage Communications process, option B describes the Manage Stakeholder Engagement process, and option D describes the Manage Quality process.

24. B. The Plan Resource Management process identifies project resources, documents roles and responsibilities of project team members, and documents reporting relationships.

25. A-4, B-1, C-3, D-5, E-2. Testing at all levels is a concept used in Extreme Programming, and other agile methodologies, to expose issues and problems early in the coding process.

26. B. The planning meeting occurs at the beginning of an iteration or sprint. Team members choose the items from the backlog that they will work on in the upcoming sprint.

27. D. Pareto diagrams rank-order important factors for corrective action by frequency of occurrence.

28. D. Team building does occur throughout the life of the project, but ground rules are what establish clear expectations and behaviors for project team members.

29. D. The payback period for Project Fish'n for Chips is eight months. This project will receive $300,000 every three months, or $100,000 per month. Project Fish'n for Chips has the shortest payback period and should be chosen over Project Picnic.

30. C. Fast-tracking is a compression technique that increases risk and potentially causes rework. Fast-tracking is performing two activities previously scheduled to start one after the other in parallel.

31. B. Inspection involves physically looking at, measuring, or testing results to determine whether they conform to your quality standards.

32. B. Functional managers who have a lot of authority and power working with project coordinators who have minimal authority and power characterizes a weak matrix organization. Project managers in weak matrix organizations are sometimes called project coordinators, project leaders, or project expeditors.

33. C. The deliverables are validated and accepted during the Validate Scope process.

34. A. The requirements documentation contains a list of requirements for the project along with other important information regarding the requirements.

35. B. The purpose of a project charter is to recognize and acknowledge the existence of a project and commit resources to the project. The charter names the project manager and project sponsor, but that's not its primary purpose.

36. A, B. Identify Stakeholders tools and techniques are expert judgment, data gathering, data analysis, data representation, and meetings. The Salience model and power/interest grid are two of the data representation techniques you can use to categorize and show stakeholder information. The stakeholder register is where the information is recorded.

37. C. Secondary risk events occur as a result of the implementation of a response to another risk.

38. C. The four types of project endings are addition, integration, starvation, and extinction.

39. B. Estimate Costs is where activity costs are estimated using some of the tools and techniques listed in the question. The remaining tools and techniques of this process are expert judgment, data analysis, project management information system, and decision-making.

40. B. Failure costs are associated with the cost of quality and are also known as cost of poor quality.

41. D. The critical chain is a resource-constrained critical path that adds duration buffers to help protect schedule slippage. For more information, please see Chapter 5.

42. A. Scope changes will cause schedule revisions, but schedule revisions do not change the project scope. Project requirements are part of the project scope statement; therefore, scope change might come about as a result of changes to the project requirements, as stated in option D.

43. D. The Determine Budget process establishes the cost baseline, which is used to measure and track the project throughout the remaining process groups.

44. C. The inputs to Develop Project Management Plan include project charter, outputs from other processes, enterprise environmental factors (EEF), and organizational process assets (OPA). The tools and techniques of this process are expert judgment, data gathering, interpersonal and team skills, and meetings.

45. A, D. This question describes a servant leader. They take three steps to ensure the team learns and matures the agile process: purpose, people, process.

46. B. Monte Carlo analysis is a simulation technique that is part of a simulation tool and technique performed in the Perform Quantitative Risk Analysis process.

47. C. VAC is calculated this way: VAC = BAC – EAC. Therefore, 525 – 500 = 25.

48. D. Fixed-price increments are contracts used on agile projects that are based on breaking down the work into user stories, rather than pricing the contract as a whole.

49. E. Risk audits should be performed throughout the life of the project, and you are specifically interested in looking at the implementation and effectiveness of risk strategies.

50. A. The two types of agile approaches discussed in the Agile Practice Guide (PMI®, 2017) are iteration-based (like Scrum) and flow-based (like Kanban).

51. D. The PMI® Code of Ethics and Professional Conduct is published by PMI®, and all PMP® credential holders are expected to adhere to its standards.

52. A. According to the PMBOK® Guide, the project manager should be assigned during the development of the project charter, which occurs in the Develop Project Charter process.

53. D. The project manager is responsible for delivering business value incrementally throughout the project, not just at the end of the project.

54. E. Risks are uncertain events that may be threats or opportunities to the objectives of the project.

55. F. Shu Ha Ri is a technique that comes from Aikido. Shu means to obey or protect, Ha means to break free or digress, and Ri means to separate or leave.

56. A-2, B-5, C-3, D-1, E-4. Scaling agile frameworks is a technique used to scale agile practices to the organization and incorporate multiple teams using agile methodologies.

57. D. Estimate at completion (EAC) estimates the total cost of the project at completion based on the performance of the project to date.

58. B. The project management Knowledge Areas bring together processes that have commonalities. For example, the Project Quality Management Knowledge Area includes the Plan Quality Management, Manage Quality, and Control Quality processes.

59. C. The tools and techniques of the Define Scope process include product analysis, alternatives analysis, expert judgment, multicriteria decision analysis, and facilitation.

60. D. All of the options are true in relation to an adaptive methodology.

61. A. Planned value is the cost of work that has been authorized and budgeted for a schedule activity or WBS component.

62. A. The Plan Risk Management process contains three tools and techniques: data analysis (stakeholder analysis), expert judgment, and meetings. Meetings are used to determine the plans for performing risk management activities. One of the key components of these meetings is to determine risk cost elements, along with schedule activities, and definitions of terms, and the development or definition of the probability and impact matrix.

63. A. Operational definitions are quality metrics. They describe what is being measured and how it will be measured during the Control Quality process.

64. D. Information that is complex and detailed is best conveyed in writing. A verbal follow-up would be good to answer questions and clarify information. Vertical and horizontal are ways of communicating within the organization.

65. A. The best response is to decline the offer. This is a conflict of interest, and accepting the offer puts your own integrity and the contract award process in jeopardy.

66. A-3, B-5, C-2, D-1, E-4. Agile projects typically follow a workflow that consists of defining the product backlog, holding planning meetings,

conducting daily stand-ups, holding review meetings, and conducting retrospectives.

67. C. Project B's cost–benefit analysis is a $9.2 million benefit to the company, compared to $6.6 million for Project A. Cost– benefit analysis takes into consideration the initial costs to implement and future operating costs.

68. B, D, E. Pondy identified five stages of conflict including latent, perceived, felt, manifest, and aftermath. Options A and C describe conflict resolution techniques.

69. C. Option C describes voting methods that are used in the decision-making tool and technique. They are not part of alternatives analysis.

70. B. Manage Quality is the process where project managers have the greatest amount of influence over quality.

71. C. Weak matrix organizational structures tend to experience the least amount of stress during the project closeout processes.

72. B, D. Business value brings short- or long-term benefits to the organization. Business value for this project is stated in the question as increasing revenues and market share. KPIs are usually numeric metrics used to examine whether business value was achieved. This project was requested by customers and the new manufacturing processes describe a technological advancement. Organization need usually entails projects focused on internal organizational needs such as upgrading a software system or finding a new building to lease.

73. C. These elements are part of the business case used as an input (through the business documents input) to the Develop Project Charter process.

74. A. Constraints limit the options of the project team by restricting action or dictating action. Scope, time, and cost are the three most common constraints, and each of these has an effect on quality. Assumptions are presumed to be true for planning purposes. Always validate your assumptions.

75. B. Achievement Theory conjectures that people are motivated by the need for achievement, power, or affiliation.

76. B. When people work in unfamiliar environments, culture shock can occur. Training and researching information about the country you'll be working in can help counteract this.

77. A. The clues in this question are the face-to-face meetings resolving issues, managing expectations, and improving project performance, which are the primary purposes of the Manage Stakeholder Engagement process. Project management plan updates include both the communications management plan and stakeholder engagement plan and are an output of this process.

78. A, C. Scrum and Extreme Programming (XP) are agile project management methodologies that are used in the information technology field.

79. B. Option A describes total float. Options C and D are incorrect.

80. C, D. Option A describes the Silent Generation and option B describes the Gen X generation.

81. B. Honesty and truthful reporting are required of PMP® credential holders. In this situation, you would inform the customer of everything you know regarding the problem and work to find alternative solutions.

82. A. The Planning process group is where requirements are fleshed out and estimates on project costs and time are made.

83. B. The components of the interactive communication model are encode, transmit, decode, acknowledge, and feedback/response. The basic communication model consists of the sender, message, and receiver elements.

84. D. The project manager is responsible for performing and managing project integration while the project team members are responsible for planning, control, and delivery of the product.

85. C. Independent estimates are also known as should cost estimates.

86. D. Risk occurrence is lowest during the Closing process group because you've completed the work of the project at this point. However, risk impacts are the greatest in the Closing process because you have much more at stake.

87. F. PESTLE is used to assist in identifying risks. The other factors you can consider that are not listed in the options are proximity, dormancy, controllability, connectivity, and strategic impact.

88. A. A conflict of interest is any situation that compromises the outcome of the project or ignores the impact to the project to benefit yourself or others.

89.C. The Project Management Institute (PMI)® is the industry recognized standard for project management practices.

90. B. Projects exist to create a unique product, service, or result. The new color line is not a unique product. A minor change has been requested (to add a new color), indicating that this is an ongoing operations function. Some of the criteria for projects are that they are unique, temporary with definitive start and end dates, and considered complete when the project goals are achieved.

91. A. This is a project. The product line is new, which implies that this is a unique product—it hasn't been done before. You can discern a definite start and end date by the fact that the new appliances must be ready by the spring catalog release.

92. B, D. You can't know the characteristics and features without consulting with the stakeholders. Progressive elaboration is the process of determining the characteristics and features of the product of the project. Progressive elaboration is carried out via steps in detailed fashion. The project was already approved, as stated in this question, so the business value should have already been defined. The project life cycle planning will start in the Planning process group of the project. You are still in the Initiating process.

93. B. This came about because of an organizational need. Staff members were spending unproductive hours producing information for the management report that wasn't consistent or meaningful.

94. C. Project management brings together a set of tools and techniques to organize project activities. Project managers are the ones responsible for managing the project management processes.

95. A, C, D. There are three ways phases can be performed in a multiphased project: sequential, iterative, and overlapping. Iterative is when more than one phase is being performed at the same time, and overlapping occurs when one phase starts before the prior phase completes. All phases should perform a phase gate review.

96. A, C, D. Option B describes the waterfall, or predictive, process.

97. B. When one business develops new pricing structures or new products, or offers more for the same, competing businesses must do something similar in order to stay competitive. This is the definition of competitive forces.

98. D. Portfolios are collections of projects and/or programs. The projects or programs do not have to be directly related or interdependent to reside within the portfolio.

99. D. The processes, in order, are Initiating, Planning, Executing, Monitoring and Controlling, and Closing.

100. C. The Initiating process group is where stakeholders have the greatest ability to influence outcomes of the project. Risk is highest during this stage because of the high degree of unknown factors.

101. B, C, D. The three types of PMOs are supportive, controlling, and directive.

102. C. The seven wastes are associated with Kaizen, a Lean methodology.

103. E, F. Scrum and Kanban are considered pull systems because user stories are moved from one point in the process to the next, thereby freeing up space to pull other user stories from the backlog.

104. B. Six Sigma relies heavily on statistical data.

105. A, C, D. The agile methodologies require close contact with the stakeholders, and this provides continuous feedback to the project team throughout the project. In a waterfall approach, stakeholders typically have a lot of contact and involvement with the team at the beginning of the project, and this involvement tapers off toward the end of the project. Option E also describes an agile methodology approach. Waterfall, or predictive, methodologies do not have iterative reviews and changes are rigorously controlled and managed.

106. B, C. The Agile Practice Guide (PMI®, 2017). focuses on value to the customer, not in measuring processes or the quality of deliverables. Success is measured in incremental steps.

107. A-3, B-1, C-4, D-2. Project and program management focuses on performing the projects in the right way, whereas portfolio management focuses on working on the right projects and programs at the right time. OPM aligns projects with the organization's strategic business objectives. The PMO is a centralized unit that oversees the management of projects throughout the organization.

108. C. This describes a hybrid development life cycle. Early on, requirements might be gathered in detail, and as the project progresses,

the team reverts to an agile approach to deliver functionality incrementally.

109.   A. OPAs are internal to the organization. EEFs can be internal or external to the organization but they are always outside the control of the project team. EEFs may include government or industry regulations and can therefore drive compliance requirements for the project.

110.   D, E. According to the PMBOK® Guide, the project charter should be issued by the project sponsor or the project initiator. Once the charter is approved, the project manager will use the goals of the project to set a clear vision and mission for the project and continually inform the team and the stakeholders of the objectives and mission of the project. It's also used to help align stakeholder expectations with the objectives of the project. Project charters are typically required when using a predictive methodology, and they may be also be used in a hybrid methodology approach.

111.   B, C. Integration is managed and performed by the project manager when using an agile methodology. The agile team is responsible for planning, delivery, and control of the product. Integration focuses on coordinating all aspects of the project, not just those mentioned in Option D. Integration can be used with any project management methodology, not just predictive.

112.   B, D. This describes the Project Schedule Management Knowledge Area, which involves the following processes: Plan Schedule Management, Define Activities, Sequence Activities, Estimate Activity Durations, Develop Schedule, and Control Schedule. The question also describes a predictive methodology. The question describes a step-by-step approach by finishing the first activity (estimating) before creating a schedule. In agile, these activities are performed together.

113.   A. The benefits management plan is created early in the project and it is updated iteratively throughout the life of the project. The business case is reviewed at each phase gate.

114.   C. The project charter is the document that names the project manager.

115.   B. Historical information on projects of a similar nature can be helpful when initiating new projects. They can help in formulating project

deliverables and identifying constraints and assumptions and will be helpful later in the project Planning processes as well.

116.   C. Procurement Management generally occurs at the beginning of the project in an agile methodology. You may have procurements at some point in the project and they may become a iteration activity, but they are not performed before, during, and after every iteration.

117.   A. Option B describes the project exit criteria. Option C is not true, and Option D is partially true. The project manager does not dictate what the approval requirements are. The stakeholders and sponsor will come to agreement on the success criteria, and the project manager may or may not have a voice in the decision.

118.   B. Projects with NPV greater than 0 should be given an accept recommendation.

119.   D. Projects with the highest IRR value are favored over projects with lower IRR values.

120.   A. Net present value (NPV) assumes reinvestment is made at the cost of capital.

121.   C. Year 1 and 2 inflows are each $100,000 for a total of $200,000. Year 3 inflows are an additional $300,000. Add one more quarter to this total, and the $575,000 is reached in three years and three months, or 39 months.

122.   D. IRR assumes reinvestment at the IRR rate and is the discount rate when NPV is equal to 0.

123.   C. The purpose of the business case is to understand the business need for the project and determine whether the investment in the project is worthwhile. This may include analysis using benefit measurement methods. The benefits, how they're measured, and how they're obtained is contained in the benefits management plan.

124.   A, D, F. The results of the needs assessment are documented in the business case. The Develop Project Charter resides in the Project Integration Management Knowledge Area.

125.   B. Project B has a payback period of 21 months; $50,000 is received in the first 12 months, with another $75,000 coming in over each of the next three quarters, or nine months.

126.   C. Payback period does not consider the time value of money and is, therefore, the least precise of all the cash flow analysis techniques.

127.   C. The project should be kicked off with a project charter that authorizes the project to begin, assigns the project manager, and describes the project objectives and purpose for the project. Doing so ensures that everyone is working with the same purposes in mind.

128.   A, B, C, E. There is not a requirement to print project documents. They should be available for future reference as historical information for future projects.

129.   D. A project is considered successful when it achieves its objectives and stakeholder needs and expectations are met.

130.   B, C. Conflicts between stakeholders should always be resolved in favor of the customer. This question emphasizes the importance of identifying your stakeholders and their needs as early as possible in the project.

131.   A, C, D. The level of authority the project manager has is determined by the organizational structure, interactions with various management levels, and the project management maturity level of the organization.

132.   A, B, E. Advantages for employees in a functional organization are that they have only one supervisor and a clear chain of command exists. Organizational structures and culture are independent from the development or life-cycle methodology you'll use to manage the project (such as predictive, adaptive, or hybrid). Adaptive and hybrid methodologies can be challenging because resources on these teams are self-organized and self-directed, which could be difficult in a functional organization. The project manager will have to work with functional managers to obtain resources for the project in this structure.

133.   D. DMAIC stands for define, measure, analyze, improve, and control. The define phase is where the project goals are established, stakeholders are identified, and the project charter is written.

134.   E. All of the options are true. Option A describes the EEFs as an input to the Identify Stakeholder process. All of these factors should be taken into consideration when assessing stakeholders.

135.   A, B. The project manager is responsible for ensuring corrective actions are taken. Change requests bring about changes, not corrective actions. However, a corrective action may bring about a change request.

136.   E. All of these are true. The business need that brought about the project is twofold, improving customer satisfaction and a business need. Customers were complaining according to the question and the business need involved implementing a new system that would in turn improve satisfaction scores. Customer satisfaction is often measured using surveys. The project manager is responsible for championing the business value for the project throughout its life cycle. An agile approach would have allowed for this change to be incorporated into a future iteration and could have averted a two-month delay.

137.   A-1, B-4, C-2, D-6, E-5, F-3. The Salience model is a tool and technique in the Identify Stakeholder process that allows you to categorize stakeholders according to power, urgency, and legitimacy.

138.   B. Business values are those values that will lead to short- and long-term benefits for the organization.

139.   A, B, D. This question describes the stakeholder register. You may have used the power/interest grid to classify your stakeholders, but this tool does not contain other information such as contact information.

140.   A-5, B-1, C-2, D-4, E-3. This question describes the various titles project managers may have in different adaptive methodologies.

141.   E. Business value involves bringing short- and -long term benefits to the organization. Creating a new car model and implementing a new accounting system are project goals, not a business value.

142.   C, D, E. The project manager is responsible for understanding the urgency required to deliver the business value of the project. The project sponsor defines the urgency, but the project manager is responsible for delivering the project according to the urgency driving the business value. Urgency is subjective and is defined by the project sponsor.

143.   A, C. You should examine and report on business value throughout the life of the project, you should always consider delivering business value incrementally whenever possible, and it's the project manager's responsibility to champion the business value of the project (not expecting others to periodically review the business value statement in the project charter).

144.   C. Key performance indicators are a way to measure business value. It is the project manger's responsibility to measure and report on value. This is objective, not subjective, like asking the project sponsor what they think.

145.   B. The business value network can include internal resources, employees, and stakeholders, not just external resources.

146.   A, D. The minimum viable product is a component of work, or a task, that's been broken down into the lowest tangible feature, function, or result possible. The product owner is responsible for determining if business value has been achieved. The project team does not manage or prioritize the backlog; the product owner does. The Scrum master is a facilitator. Team members do not report to the Scrum master, and they do not assign tasks to team members.

147.   D. All of the options are true regarding the minimum viable product.

148.   B. Adjustments, changes, and corrections can be made at any time during the iteration.

149.   A, B, D. Option C describes the project scope statement.

150.   B, C, E. Options A and D may have been considered when developing the project documents so far, but they are not reasons to hold a kickoff meeting.

151.   B, E. The scope management plan describes how project scope will be defined and validated, how the scope statement will be developed, how the WBS will be created and defined, and how project scope will be managed and controlled. Project scope is measured against the project management plan, whereas product scope is measured against the product requirements. It is based on the approved project scope. The project scope management plan defines, maintains, and manages the scope of the project.

152.   A, D. These four decision-making techniques belong to the Collect Requirements process and are part of the decision-making tool and technique in this process. They help stakeholders make decisions and come to agreement on the requirements of the project.

153.   B, C, E. The project scope statement further elaborates the project deliverables and documents the product scope description,

acceptance criteria, and project exclusions. It serves as a basis for future project decisions. It is an agreement between the project team and the customer on the precise work of the project. This question describes a hybrid approach so you could use either a project scope statement or a product backlog to compile user stories, which are the deliverables and requirements for the project. Options A and D describe the scope management plan.

154.	D. The requirements traceability matrix links requirements to their origin and traces them throughout the project. Option A describes the requirements management plan, not the requirements document. Option B is partially true, with the exception of the first statement. Requirements documents do not have to be formal or complex. Option C refers to the project scope statement, not the requirements.

155.	F. The scope baseline consists of the approved project scope statement, the WBS, and the WBS dictionary.

156.	A, B. Brainstorming and lateral thinking are not decisionmaking techniques. They are used to help generate free form ideas and create information that can later be decided on.

157.	A. You could use each product as a level one entry on the WBS, so option A is correct, but you may choose to construct the WBS differently. Option C is not correct because rolling wave planning is the process of fully elaborating near-term WBS work packages and elaborating others, like the third product in this question, at a later time when all information is known.

158.	C. Poor scope definition might lead to cost increases, rework, schedule delays, and poor morale. Option C describes the project scope management plan.

159.	D. Each element in the WBS is assigned a unique identifier called a code of accounts identifier. Typically, these codes are associated with a corporate chart of accounts and are used to track the costs of the individual work elements in the WBS.

160.	B, C, D. The work package level is the lowest level in the WBS and facilitates resource assignment and cost and time estimates. The work package level on an agile project is the user story. In this question, the work package level contains four subprojects, so it would not be used to create the activity list. The activity list will be created from the work package level for each WBS created for each subproject.

161.   C. The primary constraint is time. Since the trade show demos depend on project completion and the trade show is in late September, the date cannot be moved. The budget is the secondary constraint in this example.

162.   E. Decomposition subdivides the major deliverables into smaller components. It is a tool and technique of the Create WBS process and is used to create a WBS. In an agile methodology, user stories are the work package level of the WBS and are documented in the product backlog. They are pulled from there into the spring backlog at the beginning of the iteration and further decomposed into tasks.

163.   C, D. Acceptance criteria are documented in the project scope statement in a predictive methodology and in the user stories for an adaptive methodology.

164.   D. The primary constraint is quality. If you made the assumption as stated in options A, B, and C, you assumed incorrectly. Clarify these assumptions with your stakeholders and project sponsors.

165.   C. This is an example of an assumption. You've used this vendor before and haven't had any problems. You're assuming there will be no problems with this delivery based on your past experience.

166.   B, C. This describes a regulatory standard and/or compliance issue, which are part of the organization's EEFs. Constraints restrict the actions of the project team.

167.   A. The project came about because of a business need. The phones have to be answered because that's the core business. Upgrading the system to handle more volume is a business need. An assumption has been made regarding vendor availability. Always validate your assumptions.

168.   B. The steps of decomposition include identify major deliverables, organize and determine the structure, identify lower-level components, assign identification codes, and verify correctness of decomposition.

169.   C, D. Activity lists can be created using any tool and technique the agile team wants to use, not just the ones found in the Define Activities process. The iteration planning meeting is where the user stories are

broken into activities, but a high-level breakdown may also occur early on in the project to determine project duration estimates. These estimates may be based on story points or iterations.

170.   A, C, D. According to the PMBOK® Guide, the schedule management plan should be completed no matter what life cycle methodology you're using.

171.   C. Reserve analysis takes schedule risk into consideration and adds a percentage of time or additional work periods to the estimate to prevent schedule delays.

172.   A. Parametric estimating uses an algorithm or formula that multiplies a known element—such as the quantity of materials needed—by the time it takes to install or complete one unit of materials. The result is a total estimate for the activity. In this case, 10 servers multiplied by 16 hours per server gives you a 160-hour total duration estimate.

173.   A, B, D. The activity list is a component of the project schedule, not the WBS. The activity list includes all the project activities, an identifier, and a description of the activity. The activity list is an output of the Define Activities process.

174.   D. This is an example of a mandatory dependency, also known as hard logic. Mandatory dependencies are inherent in the nature of the work. Discretionary dependencies, also called preferred logic, preferential logic, and soft logic, are defined by the project management team.

175.   A-2, B-4, C-1, D-3. The foundational principles of the Agile Manifesto include a maximum focus on delivering value to the customer with minimum focus on the process.

176.   D. The project schedule should be easily accessible by all stakeholders, and you should notify them when there are updates. The original schedule baseline should be saved so that you can compare future changes to it.

177.   D. Finish-to-start (FS) is the most commonly used logical relationship in PDM and the default relationship in most project management software packages.

178.   C. CPM calculates a single early and late start date and a single early and late finish date for each activity. Once these dates are known,

float time is calculated for each activity to determine the critical path. The other answers contain elements of PERT calculations.

179.   B. The only information you have for this example is activity duration; therefore, the critical path is the path with the longest duration. Path A-D-E-H with a duration of 34 days is the critical path.

180.   D. The only information you have for this example is activity duration, so you must calculate the critical path based on the durations given. The duration of A-B-C-E-H increased by 3 days, for a total of 35 days. The duration of A-F-G-H and A-F-G-E-H each increased by 3 days. A-F-G-E-H totals 36 days and becomes the new critical path.

181.   D. You calculate the critical path by adding together the durations of all the tasks with zero or negative float. The critical path can be compressed using crashing techniques.

182.   C. The calculation for PERT is the sum of optimistic time plus pessimistic time plus four times the most likely time divided by

183.   The calculation for this example is as follows: (48 + 72 + (4 *60)) / 6 = 60.

184.   D. You calculate the standard deviation by subtracting the optimistic time from the pessimistic time and dividing the result by 6. The calculation for this example is as follows: (72 – 48) / 6= 4.

185.   D. There is a 95 percent probability that the work will finish within plus or minus two standard deviations. The expected value is 500, and the standard deviation times 2 is 24, so the activity will take from 476 to 524 days.

186.   B. This is known as the basis of estimates.

187.   A. Crashing the schedule includes tasks such as adding resources to the critical path tasks or speeding up deliveries of materials and resources.

188.   C. Resource leveling is used for over allocated resources and allows for changes to the schedule completion dates. Crashing and fast tracking are schedule compression techniques that shorten the schedule. Resource smoothing techniques will not allow for changes to the critical path or project end date, and since you are concerned about not overusing this resource, lengthening the schedule is a better option.

189. B, C. Velocity is used to determine how long it will take to complete the work of the iteration. It measures the speed with which the team progresses, not capacity. Kanban boards display work based on capacity. Velocity is time bound.

190. B, C. The communications management plan, not the stakeholder engagement plan, defines and manages the flow of project information. The communications management plan also documents the types of information needs the stakeholders have, when the information should be distributed, how the information will be delivered, and how communications will be monitored and controlled throughout the project. The communications management plan considers the organizational structure and stakeholder requirements. The stakeholder engagement plan captures the strategies needed to engage stakeholders throughout the project and to assist in decisionmaking and project execution.

191. A, D. The cost management plan, an output of the Plan Cost Management process, is developed by considering the project scope, schedule, resources, and the approved project charter. The level of precision and accuracy and the units of measure and control thresholds are included in the cost management plan.

192. D. Control thresholds are variance thresholds (typically stated as a percentage of deviation from the baseline) used for monitoring cost performance.

193. C. The cost management plan is established using the WBS and its associated control accounts. A control account can be placed at any level of the WBS and is used for earned value measurement calculations regarding project costs.

194. A. Scope definition is the key component of determining cost estimates. It should be completed early in the project because costs are more easily influenced at the beginning of the project.

195. B. Three-point estimating can improve activity cost estimates because it factors in estimation uncertainty and risk.

196. B, D. Option A describes a review meeting and option C describes a retrospective meeting.

197. E. All of the options are true regarding mentoring stakeholders and ensuring buy-in for the project.

198.   A, B, D. Future period operating costs are considered ongoing costs and are not part of project costs.

199.   A, C, D. Stakeholders are classified in the stakeholder register. The neutral classification is when stakeholders neither support nor resist the project. Resistant stakeholders are not supportive of the project and may actively resist engaging. Neither of these classifications describes an adaptive methodology.

200.   B, C, D. Funding limit reconciliation concerns reconciling the funds to be spent on the project, with funding limits placed on the funding commitments for the project.

Conclusion

Preparing for the PMP (Project Management Professional) Certification Exam is a journey that demands diligence, commitment, and strategic focus. It's more than just absorbing facts; it's about understanding the nuances of project management as defined by PMI and being able to apply this knowledge in varied scenarios. From the intricate details of the PMBOK® Guide to the broader principles of the PMI Code of Ethics and Professional Conduct, every facet of your preparation carries weight.

As you embark on this intellectual voyage, remember that success hinges not just on memorizing content, but on cultivating a deep, intrinsic understanding of project management practices. Embrace a holistic approach: study systematically, engage in consistent practice with mock tests, and develop a keen analytical mindset to dissect complex questions. Lean on the aforementioned tips when answering questions and always remain attuned to PMI's perspective.

Additionally, interweave your learning with real-world experiences. Theoretical knowledge, when underpinned by practical insights, tends to be more enduring and insightful. Surround yourself with a supportive community of fellow aspirants and mentors; their shared experiences can offer invaluable insights and motivation.

In the end, while the PMP certification is a testament to your expertise in project management, the journey of preparation itself is equally transformative. It instills discipline, sharpens analytical skills, and reinforces the importance of ethical considerations in professional undertakings. As you step forward, armed with knowledge and strategies, remember that this exam is not just a test of your memory but a validation of your capability as a project manager. Forge ahead with confidence, tenacity, and the unwavering belief that your efforts will culminate in success. Good luck, and may your project management journey be both enlightening and rewarding!